MW01268859

A GUIDE TO THE
EV CHARGING
BUSINESS

Dr. Maxwell Shimba

Copyright © 2024 – Dr. Maxwell Shimba
All rights reserved. No portion of this book may be
reproduced, stored in a retrieval system, or transmitted in any
form or by any means – electronics, mechanical, photocopy,
recording, scanning, or other – except for brief quotations in
critical reviews or articles, without the prior written permission
of the publisher.

Published in Manhattan, New York by Shimba Publishing,
LLC.

Shimba Publishing, LLC
Printed in the United States of America

First Printing Edition, 2024

ISBN: 9798873893423

TABLE OF CONTENTS

INTRODUCTION

In the inexorable march towards a sustainable and electrified future, the role of electric vehicles (EVs) stands prominently at the forefront of innovation. As the automotive landscape undergoes a transformative shift, so does the infrastructure that powers this evolution. "The Future of EV Charging" is an immersive exploration into the dynamic realm of electric vehicle charging, unraveling its intricate past, decoding the present landscape, and forecasting the compelling future that lies ahead.

The journey commences with a historical odyssey, tracing the emergence of experimental electric carriages in the mid-19th century. Pioneers like Thomas Parker and Gustave Trouvé take center stage, their contributions serving as foundational stones in the narrative of early electric vehicle development. We navigate through the bustling streets of cities like London and Paris, witnessing the introduction of electric taxis and delivery vehicles, marking a significant chapter in the urban integration of EVs.

Chapter by chapter, the book unfolds the technological tapestry of EV charging. From the various types of charging stations — Level 1, Level 2, and DC fast chargers — to the intricacies of charging connectors and standards, readers are guided through the evolving landscape of charging technology. Smart charging solutions, an essential facet of the contemporary charging infrastructure, are unraveled, showcasing how connectivity and data analytics are shaping the future of electric mobility.

Delving deeper, the book explores market trends and opportunities, dissecting the global growth of the EV market, dissecting government incentives, and unearthing the vast business prospects within the EV charging industry. It's a comprehensive journey into the driving forces behind the surge in EV demand, the importance of government incentives and regulations, and the significant investments in charging infrastructure.

The subsequent chapters offer a blueprint for those seeking to venture into the world of EV charging. From planning and strategizing an EV charging business to the intricacies of building and managing charging stations, the book serves as a guide for entrepreneurs, investors, and policymakers navigating the burgeoning EV ecosystem.

Through case studies and success stories, the book introduces readers to industry trailblazers, providing insights into their strategies, innovations, and the challenges they've overcome. The appendix acts as a valuable resource, offering additional reading materials, useful websites, and a glossary of terms to assist both novices and seasoned enthusiasts in navigating the evolving language of EV charging.

"The Future of EV Charging" is not just a book; it's a roadmap to an electrified future, a future where sustainable transportation is not merely a concept but an everyday reality. As electric vehicles continue to reshape the automotive landscape, this book serves as a guiding beacon, illuminating the path towards a future where EV charging infrastructure is seamlessly integrated into the fabric of our daily lives.

DR. MAXWELL SHIMBA

CHAPTER 01

INTRODUCTION TO ELECTRIC VEHICLES

Welcome to the electrifying world of electric vehicles (EVs), where innovation, sustainability, and a cleaner future intersect. In this introduction, we embark on a journey to explore the fundamental aspects of EVs, witnessing their rapid ascent in popularity, understanding the significant environmental benefits they bring, and recognizing the crucial role of an extensive EV charging infrastructure in supporting their widespread adoption.

Electric vehicles represent a revolutionary shift in transportation, challenging traditional notions and reshaping the automotive landscape. From the early experiments in the 19th century to the cutting-edge technology of today, EVs have come a long way, driven by advancements in battery technology, electric motors, and a growing commitment to sustainability.

The surge in popularity of electric vehicles is palpable, driven by a global awareness of environmental issues, a desire for energy independence, and the allure of cutting-edge technology. As the automotive industry undergoes a transformation, electric vehicles have transitioned from niche options to mainstream choices for consumers worldwide.

Beyond the hype, the environmental benefits of electric vehicles form a compelling narrative. From a significant reduction in greenhouse gas emissions to improved air quality in urban areas, EVs play a pivotal role in addressing climate change and promoting sustainable living. They represent a departure from the reliance on fossil fuels, offering a cleaner and more efficient alternative for personal and public transportation.

However, the full realization of the electric vehicle revolution hinges on a critical component: a well-established and accessible EV charging infrastructure. This infrastructure is the backbone that alleviates concerns about range, fosters confidence among users, and propels the widespread adoption of electric mobility. Governments, businesses, and communities are investing in charging networks to bridge gaps and propel us toward a future where charging an electric vehicle is as seamless as filling a gas tank.

As we navigate through the chapters ahead, we will delve deeper into the historical roots of electric vehicles, explore the environmental advantages they bring, and analyze the pivotal role played by charging infrastructure. This exploration aims to provide you with a comprehensive understanding of electric vehicles, empowering you to navigate the exciting landscape of sustainable transportation and contribute to the future of mobility. Let's embark on this electrifying journey together.

The Rise of Electric Vehicles can be attributed to a combination of historical developments, overcoming early adoption challenges, a transformative moment spearheaded by Tesla, and the subsequent diversification of electric vehicle (EV) models from various manufacturers.

1. The History of Electric Vehicles:

- The concept of electric vehicles dates back to the 19th century, with inventors experimenting with early electric propulsion.

- Early electric vehicles saw popularity, especially in the late 1800s and early 1900s, driven by innovations in electric motors and batteries.

2. Early Adoption Challenges:

- EVs faced challenges such as limited range, lack of charging infrastructure, high production costs, and public misconceptions.

- The decline of EVs occurred due to these challenges, leading to the dominance of internal combustion engine vehicles.

3. The Turning Point: Tesla and the Electric Revolution:

- Tesla, founded by Elon Musk, played a pivotal role in redefining the narrative around electric vehicles.

- The introduction of the Tesla Roadster marked a turning point, showcasing the potential of high-performance electric cars.

- Breakthroughs in battery technology, exemplified by Tesla's Gigafactories, contributed to increased range and efficiency.

4. The Expanding Range of EV Models from Various Manufacturers:

- Competition and innovation among various automakers have led to a diverse range of electric vehicle models.

- Automakers globally have embraced electrification, introducing electric SUVs, crossovers, luxury cars, and even commercial electric vehicles.

The synergy of historical foundations, overcoming initial hurdles, Tesla's visionary approach, and the subsequent industry-wide embrace of electric mobility has fueled the rise of electric vehicles. As technology advances, charging infrastructure expands, and more manufacturers invest in electrification, electric vehicles are becoming increasingly accessible, appealing, and integral to the future of sustainable transportation.

The Environmental Benefits of Electric Vehicles are multifaceted, contributing significantly to sustainability and addressing environmental challenges. Here are key aspects of these benefits:

1. Reduction in Greenhouse Gas Emissions:

- Electric vehicles produce lower or zero tailpipe emissions, reducing the overall carbon footprint of transportation.

- The shift from internal combustion engines to electric propulsion helps mitigate climate change by lowering greenhouse gas emissions, especially carbon dioxide (CO_2).

2. Improved Air Quality in Urban Areas:

- EVs produce no tailpipe pollutants, leading to improved air quality in urban environments.

- Reduction in emissions of pollutants such as nitrogen oxides (NOx) and particulate matter contributes to better respiratory health and a cleaner atmosphere.

3. Decreased Dependence on Fossil Fuels:

- Electric vehicles decrease reliance on finite fossil fuel resources, promoting energy diversification.

- The transition to electricity as a power source allows for increased integration of renewable energy, further reducing environmental impact.

4. Energy Efficiency of Electric Propulsion:

- Electric motors are inherently more efficient than internal combustion engines, converting a higher percentage of energy from the power source to vehicle movement.

- Regenerative braking in electric vehicles captures and reuses energy during deceleration, enhancing overall energy efficiency.

These environmental benefits collectively contribute to a more sustainable and eco-friendly transportation system. Electric vehicles play a vital role in addressing environmental concerns, aligning with global efforts to reduce pollution, combat climate change, and transition to cleaner and greener forms of mobility.

The Need for EV Charging Infrastructure is imperative for several reasons, underscoring its pivotal role in the successful adoption and sustained growth of electric vehicles (EVs). Here's why:

1. Understanding Charging Infrastructure Gaps:

- Charging infrastructure gaps, where the availability of charging stations does not meet the increasing demand for electric vehicles, can hinder adoption.

- A well-distributed and accessible charging network is essential to eliminate barriers and provide a seamless experience for EV users.

2. Overcoming Range Anxiety:

- Range anxiety, the fear of running out of battery power before reaching a charging station, is a significant psychological barrier for potential EV adopters.

- An extensive and reliable charging infrastructure alleviates range anxiety by ensuring that charging stations are strategically placed, providing confidence for EV drivers.

3. Government Initiatives and Policies Promoting EV Charging:

- Governments worldwide are implementing initiatives and policies to promote EV adoption, often including financial incentives and regulations to encourage the development of charging infrastructure.

- Subsidies, tax credits, and grants incentivize businesses and communities to invest in charging stations, fostering infrastructure growth.

4. The Role of Public and Private Sectors in Infrastructure Development:

- Collaboration between the public and private sectors is crucial for the rapid development of a robust charging infrastructure.

- Public investments in infrastructure, combined with private businesses' innovation and expertise, contribute to the expansion and maintenance of charging networks.

In summary, an effective EV Charging Infrastructure is imperative to bridge gaps in accessibility, address psychological barriers like range anxiety, and align with government initiatives promoting sustainable transportation.

The collaboration between the public and private sectors plays a pivotal role in ensuring the infrastructure is widespread, reliable, and capable of supporting the growing demand for electric mobility.

The Early Adoption Challenges of electric vehicles (EVs) were substantial hurdles that impeded their widespread acceptance. These challenges included:

1. Range Limitations and Battery Technology Constraints:

- Early electric vehicles faced limitations in travel distance per charge, impacting their practicality for long journeys.

- Battery technology constraints, such as lower energy density and longer charging times, contributed to perceived inadequacies in range and convenience.

2. Lack of Charging Infrastructure:

- A scarcity of charging infrastructure, including a lack of public charging stations, made it inconvenient for users to recharge their electric vehicles.

- Limited charging options heightened concerns about range anxiety, discouraging potential EV adopters.

3. High Production Costs:

- The cost of manufacturing electric vehicles, especially the production of advanced batteries, was initially high.

- Higher upfront costs for consumers made EVs less economically competitive compared to traditional internal combustion engine vehicles.

4. Limited Public Awareness and Misconceptions about EVs:

- Lack of public awareness about the benefits and capabilities of electric vehicles contributed to a reluctance to adopt them.

- Misconceptions about EVs, including concerns about performance, reliability, and overall feasibility, hindered their acceptance among consumers.

These challenges, though significant, prompted advancements in technology, infrastructure development, and public awareness campaigns. Overcoming these early hurdles has been crucial in transforming electric vehicles from a niche market to a viable and increasingly popular transportation choice.

The Turning Point in the adoption and perception of electric vehicles can be attributed to the vision and innovations brought forth by Tesla, Inc. Several key milestones mark this transformative period:

1. The Founding and Vision of Tesla, Inc. (2003):

- Tesla, founded by Martin Eberhard and Marc Tarpenning in 2003, was later joined by Elon Musk. Musk became a major investor and assumed a leadership role in 2004.

- Elon Musk's vision for Tesla was not only to produce electric vehicles but to redefine the entire automotive industry by making sustainable transportation compelling and accessible.

2. Introduction of the Tesla Roadster (2008):

- The introduction of the Tesla Roadster in 2008 marked a significant moment. It was the first high-performance electric sports car with an impressive range, challenging the perception of EVs as slow and limited in range.

- The success of the Roadster demonstrated that electric vehicles could be desirable, not just for their environmental benefits but for their performance and innovation.

3. Breakthroughs in Battery Technology (e.g., Gigafactories):

- Tesla's investments in battery technology, notably through Gigafactories, played a pivotal role in addressing one of the critical challenges – range limitations.

- Gigafactories, large-scale production facilities for batteries, enabled Tesla to achieve economies of scale, reducing the cost of batteries and increasing their energy density.

4. The Model S, Model 3, Model X, and Model Y (2012 onwards):

- The introduction of the Model S in 2012 marked Tesla's entry into the luxury sedan market, providing long-range capabilities and setting new standards for electric vehicle performance.

- The subsequent release of the more affordable Model 3 in 2017 made electric vehicles accessible to a broader market segment.

- The Model X (SUV) and Model Y (crossover) further diversified Tesla's offerings, appealing to different consumer preferences.

Tesla's impact on the electric vehicle market has been transformative. By successfully merging cutting-edge technology, performance, and sustainability, Tesla challenged industry norms, reshaping public perception and encouraging other automakers to accelerate their efforts in electric vehicle development. Tesla's approach became a catalyst, marking the turning point that accelerated the global shift towards electric mobility.

The Expanding Range of Electric Vehicle (EV) Models from Various Manufacturers is crucial for several reasons, reflecting the evolution of the electric mobility landscape:

1. Competition and Innovation Among Automakers:

- The growing number of EV models reflects intense competition and innovation among automakers. This competition encourages continuous advancements in technology, design, and features.

- Rivalry in the electric vehicle market fosters improvements in efficiency, performance, and affordability, benefiting consumers and driving the industry forward.

2. Introduction of Electric SUVs, Crossovers, and Commercial Vehicles:

- The expansion beyond traditional electric car models to include SUVs, crossovers, and commercial vehicles addresses diverse consumer needs and preferences.

- Electric SUVs and crossovers cater to families and individuals seeking larger, versatile vehicles, while electric commercial vehicles contribute to the electrification of fleets, reducing emissions in various industries.

3. Diverse Range of EV Options, from Luxury to Affordable Models:

- The availability of electric vehicles across different price ranges broadens accessibility for consumers. Affordable models make EVs more inclusive and attainable for a larger segment of the population.

- Luxury electric vehicles showcase cutting-edge technology and performance, attracting consumers seeking premium options, contributing to the overall acceptance of electric mobility.

4. Global Shift Toward Electrification in the Automotive Industry:

- The expanding range of EV models reflects a broader global shift toward electrification in the automotive industry. Governments, manufacturers, and consumers are increasingly recognizing the importance of sustainable transportation.

- This shift aligns with environmental goals, addresses concerns about climate change, and supports the reduction of greenhouse gas emissions associated with traditional combustion engine vehicles.

In summary, the variety of electric vehicle models from different manufacturers is crucial for fostering healthy competition, meeting diverse consumer demands, and driving the global transition toward sustainable and electrified transportation. This expansion not only benefits individual consumers but also contributes to the broader goal of creating a more sustainable and environmentally friendly automotive industry.

The origins of electric propulsion in the 19th century trace back to the pioneering experiments conducted by visionaries such as Robert Anderson and Thomas Davenport. This period witnessed the inception of electrically propelled vehicles, laying the groundwork for subsequent innovations. Key aspects include:

1. Experiments by Visionary Inventors:

- Robert Anderson, a Scottish inventor, is credited with one of the earliest experiments involving electric propulsion in the early 19th century. His work involved non-rechargeable cells, and while not intended for vehicles, it contributed to the understanding of electricity.

- Thomas Davenport, an American inventor, played a crucial role in the early development of electric motors. His experiments in the 1830s led to the creation of the first practical electric motor, setting the stage for its application in various devices, including vehicles.

2. Innovations in Electric Motors and Batteries:

- Throughout the 19th century, inventors and scientists made significant strides in improving electric motors and batteries.

- Innovations in electromagnetic principles and the development of rechargeable batteries, such as the Daniell cell and the Grove cell, contributed to the advancement of electric propulsion technology.

3. Development of the First Practical Electric Vehicle Prototypes:

- Building upon these innovations, the mid-19th century witnessed the emergence of the first practical electric vehicle prototypes.

- Experimenters like Thomas Parker and Gustave Trouvé contributed to the development of early electric carriages, marking a transition from theoretical concepts to tangible applications of electric propulsion.

This period laid the foundation for the application of electric power in transportation, marking the nascent stages of what would eventually become the electric vehicle revolution. The experimentation and innovations of these early inventors set the stage for subsequent advancements, ultimately shaping the trajectory of electric mobility in the 19th century and beyond.

The experiments by visionary inventors in the 19th century were instrumental in laying the groundwork for electric propulsion. Two notable figures and their pioneering work include:

1. Robert Anderson's Pioneering Work (1830s):

- Overview: Robert Anderson, a Scottish inventor, conducted pioneering work in the 1830s, contributing to the early development of electric propulsion.

- Key Contribution: Anderson is credited with experimenting with non-rechargeable batteries during this period. While his work wasn't specifically geared towards electric vehicles, his experimentation with batteries marked an early exploration of electric power.

2. Thomas Davenport's Invention of the Practical Electric Motor:

- Overview: Thomas Davenport, an American inventor, made significant contributions to electric propulsion during the same timeframe.

- Key Contribution: In the 1830s, Davenport invented the first practical electric motor. This invention played a crucial role in making electric power more applicable for various applications, including its use in the early electric vehicle prototypes.

These experiments laid the groundwork for understanding the principles of electric power and propulsion. Anderson's work with batteries and Davenport's invention of the practical electric motor were pivotal steps that would eventually lead to the application of electric power in transportation, marking the early stages of what would evolve into the electric vehicle revolution.

Innovations in Electric Motors and Batteries

Electric Motors:

1. Evolution of Electric Motors:

- The journey of electric motors began with simple electromagnetic devices in the 19th century.

- Innovators initially employed basic designs, but over time, engineers and scientists refined these motors, enhancing their efficiency and performance.

2. Advancements in Design:

- Through the 19th and 20th centuries, the design of electric motors evolved significantly.

- Innovators explored improvements in magnetic materials, coil configurations, and overall motor construction to maximize efficiency and power output.

3. Transition to More Efficient Designs:

- Technological advancements led to the development of more efficient electric motor designs.

- Innovations like brushless DC motors and advancements in control systems increased efficiency, reduced energy losses, and expanded the practical applications of electric motors.

Batteries:

1. Advancements in Battery Technology:

   - Battery technology underwent transformative advancements, particularly in the 19th and 20th centuries.

   - Innovations were driven by the need for more reliable and efficient energy storage solutions, especially for portable and mobile applications.

2. Introduction of Rechargeable Batteries:

   - The Daniell cell, introduced in the 1830s, was an early example of a rechargeable battery that utilized copper and zinc electrodes in a liquid electrolyte.

   - The Grove cell, another notable innovation, further improved rechargeable battery technology with a combination of zinc and platinum electrodes.

3. Development of Secondary Batteries:

   - The late 19th and early 20th centuries saw the emergence of secondary batteries, capable of being recharged multiple times.

   - Innovations like the lead-acid battery and nickel-cadmium battery represented significant steps forward in rechargeable battery technology.

4. Contemporary Lithium-ion Technology:

   - The latter half of the 20th century and into the 21st century witnessed the dominance of lithium-ion batteries.

- Lithium-ion batteries, with their high energy density and relatively low weight, became a cornerstone in powering various applications, including electric vehicles.

These innovations in electric motors and batteries have been pivotal in enabling the widespread adoption of electric propulsion. From enhanced motor efficiency to the development of rechargeable batteries, these advancements continue to shape the landscape of electric vehicles and portable electronics, driving the transition towards more sustainable and efficient technologies.

Development of the First Practical Electric Vehicle Prototypes

1. Emergence of Experimental Electric Carriages (Mid-19th Century):

- The mid-19th century witnessed a significant shift from theoretical concepts to tangible applications of electric propulsion.

- Experimental electric carriages, often resembling horse-drawn carriages, emerged as pioneers explored the feasibility of electric power for transportation.

2. Notable Pioneers in Early Electric Vehicles:

- Thomas Parker:

- Contribution: Thomas Parker, a British inventor, was a notable figure in the development of early electric vehicles.

- Innovation: Parker played a key role in creating one of the first practical electric vehicles, a tram, which was deployed in Wales in the late 1880s.

- Gustave Trouvé:

- Contribution: Gustave Trouvé, a French inventor, was another pioneer in the field of electric transportation.

- Innovation: Trouvé developed various electric vehicles, including a three-wheeled electric carriage showcased at the Paris Exposition in 1881, demonstrating the potential of electric propulsion.

3. Introduction of Electric Taxis and Delivery Vehicles:

- In the late 19th century, electric vehicles found practical applications in urban settings, particularly for public transportation and delivery services.

- Electric Taxis in London:

- Electric taxis, such as those introduced in London in the late 19th century, provided a cleaner alternative to horse-drawn cabs, contributing to efforts to address urban pollution.

- Electric Delivery Vehicles in Paris:

- In cities like Paris, electric delivery vehicles started to replace horse-drawn wagons, offering a quieter and more environmentally friendly solution for urban logistics.

4. Challenges and Advances:

- Challenges: Early electric vehicles faced challenges such as limited range, battery constraints, and competition from internal combustion engine vehicles.

- Advances: Despite challenges, these pioneers laid the groundwork for future advancements, showcasing the viability of electric vehicles in certain applications and spurring further innovations.

The development of these early electric vehicle prototypes marked a crucial phase in transportation history, demonstrating the feasibility of electric power for practical use. The experimentation and innovations during this period set the stage for the ongoing evolution of electric mobility, leading to the diverse range of electric vehicles we see today.

CHAPTER 02

EV CHARGING TECHNOLOGY

EV Charging Technology: Navigating the Future of Electric Mobility

Welcome to the intricacies of EV Charging Technology, where innovation meets the growing demand for sustainable and efficient transportation. In this exploration, we embark on a journey through the various facets of charging technology that are shaping the landscape of electric vehicle (EV) charging.

1. Types of Charging Stations:

- Level 1 Charging: Unveiling the simplicity of basic household charging and its applications for residential and workplace settings.

- Level 2 Charging: Delving into the capabilities of Level 2 charging stations, both in residential and public environments, and their pivotal role in daily EV usage.

- DC Fast Chargers: Exploring the high-speed convenience of DC fast chargers, designed for on-the-go charging in diverse scenarios, from long-distance travel to urban environments.

2. Charging Connectors and Standards:

- Introduction to Charging Connectors: Understanding the array of connectors used in EV charging and their influence on compatibility.

- Charging Standards: Unraveling the world of global charging standards, ensuring interoperability and fostering a seamless charging experience. Witness the evolution of standards in response to technological advancements.

3. Smart Charging Solutions:

- The Concept of Smart Charging: Defining smart charging in the context of electric vehicles and its integration with the smart grid and renewable energy sources.

- Benefits of Smart Charging: Exploring the advantages of smart charging, including energy optimization, cost savings, and its role in demand response for grid stability.

- Technological Innovations: Introducing emerging technologies in smart charging, from vehicle-to-grid capabilities to bidirectional charging, shaping the future of interactive and intelligent charging solutions.

This journey into EV Charging Technology is not just a technical exploration but a glimpse into the transformative potential that these innovations hold. As we embrace the evolution from traditional charging to the dynamic landscape of smart solutions, the way we power electric vehicles is becoming not just a functional aspect but an integral part of a sustainable and connected future. Join us as we navigate this exciting realm where technology meets mobility, setting the stage for a cleaner and smarter tomorrow.

The types of charging stations for electric vehicles can be categorized based on the charging power and speed. Here are the main types:

1. Level 1 Charging:

- Description: Level 1 charging stations are basic charging points that use a standard household electrical outlet.

- Power Output: Typically provides 120 volts AC (alternating current).

- Charging Speed: Relatively slow, suitable for overnight charging.

- Applications: Commonly used for residential charging and workplace charging where vehicles are parked for an extended period.

2. Level 2 Charging:

- Description: Level 2 charging stations offer a higher power output compared to Level 1 and require dedicated charging equipment.

- Power Output: Typically provides 240 volts AC.

- Charging Speed: Faster than Level 1, suitable for daily charging needs.

- Applications: Widely used in public charging stations, commercial spaces, and at home for faster charging.

3. DC Fast Chargers (Level 3):

- Description: DC fast chargers provide high-voltage direct current (DC) power directly to the vehicle's battery.

- Power Output: Varies but can go up to 800 volts DC.

- Charging Speed: Rapid charging, significantly faster than Level 1 and Level 2.

- Applications: Suited for quick charging along highways, at charging stations in urban areas, and for long-distance travel.

Each type of charging station serves different charging needs and scenarios, catering to the diverse requirements of electric vehicle users. The combination of these charging options contributes to the flexibility and accessibility of electric vehicle charging infrastructure.

Level 1 Charging: Unveiling the Basics

Introduction to Basic Household Charging:

Level 1 charging represents the foundational layer of electric vehicle (EV) charging, utilizing standard household electrical outlets for the charging process. In this introduction, we explore the fundamental aspects of Level 1 charging and its applications in various settings.

Overview of Level 1 Charging Stations:

1. Power Output: Level 1 charging typically operates on a standard 120-volt alternating current (VAC) electrical system.

2. Charging Speed: The charging speed for Level 1 is relatively slow compared to higher-level chargers, making it suitable for overnight charging scenarios.

3. Applications: Level 1 charging stations are commonly found in residential settings and workplaces where vehicles are parked for extended periods, allowing for gradual charging over time.

Considerations for Residential and Workplace Charging:

1. Residential Charging: Level 1 charging is well-suited for home charging, especially in scenarios where dedicated home charging equipment is not available. While slower than other options, it is sufficient for overnight charging, ensuring the vehicle is ready for daily use.

2. Workplace Charging: Level 1 charging can be practical in workplace settings where employees have the opportunity to park for extended periods. It provides a convenient solution for maintaining a charge during the workday, supporting the adoption of electric vehicles in corporate environments.

Understanding the basics of Level 1 charging sets the stage for a comprehensive exploration of electric vehicle charging infrastructure. While not designed for rapid charging, Level 1 charging stations play a crucial role in making electric vehicle ownership accessible and convenient, especially in residential and workplace contexts.

Level 2 Charging: Empowering Electric Mobility

Expanding on Level 2 Charging Capabilities:

Level 2 charging marks a significant advancement in electric vehicle (EV) charging capabilities, providing higher power outputs and faster charging speeds than Level 1. Let's delve into the features, benefits, and crucial aspects of Level 2 charging.

Features and Benefits for Residential and Public Charging Infrastructure:

1. Power Output: Level 2 charging stations typically operate at 240 volts alternating current (VAC), allowing for a more potent and efficient charging process compared to Level 1.

2. Charging Speed: The increased power output results in a faster charging speed, making Level 2 charging suitable for various scenarios, including daily use.

3. Residential Charging: Level 2 charging stations are commonly installed at homes, providing a practical solution for EV owners who want faster charging without the need for high-voltage equipment. This is particularly valuable for households with multiple EVs or when quick top-ups are desired.

4. Public Charging Infrastructure: Level 2 charging is widely deployed in public charging stations, offering a balance between charging speed and infrastructure cost. This makes it suitable for locations where drivers may park for an extended period, such as shopping centers, workplaces, and public parking lots.

The Role of Level 2 Charging in Daily EV Usage:

1. Convenience for Daily Charging: Level 2 charging is well-suited for daily use, ensuring that EVs can be charged conveniently and reliably.

2. Supporting EV Adoption: The faster charging speed of Level 2 contributes to the overall convenience of electric vehicles, making them a more practical choice for a broader range of drivers.

3. Extended Range Maintenance: Level 2 charging is effective for maintaining an EV's charge during daily routines, supporting longer commutes or additional trips without the concern of running out of power.

Level 2 charging stations play a pivotal role in enhancing the practicality of electric vehicles, offering faster charging speeds compared to Level 1 while maintaining versatility for both residential and public charging infrastructure. This advancement contributes to the broader adoption of electric mobility in daily life.

DC Fast Chargers: Powering Ahead for Convenience

Unveiling the Significance of DC Fast Chargers:

DC fast chargers stand as the pinnacle of electric vehicle (EV) charging technology, offering high-speed charging that caters to the needs of on-the-go drivers. In this exploration, we uncover the significance of DC fast chargers and their transformative impact on the EV charging landscape.

High-Speed Charging for On-the-Go Convenience:

1. Power Output: DC fast chargers deliver a substantial power boost, providing a direct current (DC) flow to the EV's battery.

2. Charging Speed: The high-speed charging capability significantly reduces charging times compared to Level 1 and Level 2 chargers, making it ideal for drivers seeking quick top-ups during their journeys.

3. On-the-Go Convenience: DC fast chargers are strategically positioned along highways and in urban areas, allowing drivers to rapidly charge their EVs and continue their journeys with minimal interruptions.

Applications in Long-Distance Travel and Urban Environments:

1. Long-Distance Travel: DC fast chargers play a crucial role in supporting long-distance travel for electric vehicles. Drivers can access fast charging stations strategically placed along major travel routes, reducing the time required for recharging during extended journeys.

2. Urban Environments: In urban settings where quick turnaround times are essential, DC fast chargers are deployed to cater to the needs of drivers with limited time for charging. These chargers are often found in public areas, parking lots, and commercial districts.

3. Charging Hubs: DC fast chargers are central components of EV charging hubs, providing a comprehensive solution for drivers undertaking longer trips. These hubs are designed to offer multiple fast charging stations, amenities, and services for EV users.

DC fast chargers are instrumental in addressing the range anxiety associated with electric vehicles, making long-distance travel more accessible and convenient. Their deployment in urban environments ensures that EVs remain practical for daily use, contributing to the ongoing shift towards sustainable and efficient transportation. As technology continues to advance, DC fast chargers stand as a testament to the rapid evolution of electric vehicle charging infrastructure.

Charging Connectors and Standards: Bridging the EV Charging Landscape

Electric vehicle (EV) charging relies on a variety of connectors and standards to ensure interoperability and a seamless charging experience. Let's explore the essential elements that bridge the diverse EV charging landscape.

1. Introduction to Charging Connectors:

- Diverse Connector Types: Different EV manufacturers and regions adopt various connector types. Common examples include CCS (Combined Charging System), CHAdeMO, and Tesla connectors.

- Influence on Compatibility: The design of charging connectors directly influences compatibility between charging stations and electric vehicles.

2. Charging Standards:

- Global Standards: To facilitate a universal charging experience, global standards have emerged. Examples include:

- CCS (Combined Charging System): Adopted by many automakers, CCS combines AC and DC charging in a single connector, providing flexibility for different charging scenarios.

- CHAdeMO: Particularly prevalent in Japanese and European vehicles, CHAdeMO is a fast-charging standard supporting DC charging.

- Tesla Supercharger: While Tesla vehicles use a proprietary connector, Tesla Supercharger stations are designed for Tesla vehicles, enabling rapid charging.

- Ensuring Interoperability: These standards ensure that EVs can charge at various public charging stations, regardless of the vehicle's brand or origin.

3. Evolution of Standards:

- Adaptation to Technological Advancements: Charging standards continually evolve to accommodate technological advancements in electric vehicle technology.

- Future-Proofing: The ongoing development of standards aims to future-proof charging infrastructure, supporting higher charging speeds and innovative features.

Understanding charging connectors and standards is essential for the widespread adoption of electric vehicles. As the industry continues to evolve, these connectors and standards play a pivotal role in providing a seamless and standardized charging experience for EV users around the world.

Introduction to Charging Connectors: Powering the Connection

In the intricate dance of electric vehicle (EV) charging, charging connectors take center stage, defining the interface between the vehicle and the charging infrastructure. This introduction unveils the vital role of charging connectors, providing an overview of their diversity and the key factors shaping their design and compatibility.

Overview of Connectors Used in EV Charging:

1. Diverse Connector Types: The electric vehicle landscape features a variety of connectors, each associated with specific charging standards. Common examples include CCS (Combined Charging System), CHAdeMO, and Tesla connectors.

2. AC and DC Charging: Connectors are designed to handle both Alternating Current (AC) and Direct Current (DC) charging. This versatility enables EVs to charge at different power levels and across various charging networks.

3. Proprietary and Standard Connectors: While some manufacturers adopt proprietary connectors (e.g., Tesla Supercharger), global efforts are underway to establish standardized connectors (e.g., CCS and CHAdeMO) for broader compatibility.

Key Factors Influencing Connector Design and Compatibility:

1. Voltage and Current Requirements: Connectors are tailored to meet the voltage and current requirements of specific charging standards. DC fast chargers, for instance, require connectors capable of handling higher power outputs.

2. Physical Design and Form Factor: Connectors vary in physical design, with some standards employing a single, unified connector for both AC and DC charging (e.g., CCS), while others maintain separate connectors for each (e.g., Type 2 for AC and CCS for DC).

3. Temperature and Safety Considerations: Connectors are engineered with safety in mind, incorporating features to manage temperature during charging and ensure secure connections.

4. International Standards: The push for international charging standards, such as those developed by organizations like the International Electrotechnical Commission (IEC), plays a crucial role in promoting interoperability and creating a consistent charging experience worldwide.

As we navigate the electrified future, charging connectors emerge as the unsung heroes, facilitating the crucial link between vehicles and the charging infrastructure. Their design and compatibility considerations pave the way for a seamless and universally accessible EV charging experience.

Charging Standards: The Global Tapestry of EV Charging Harmony

Examination of Global Charging Standards:

1. CCS (Combined Charging System):

   - Overview: A widely adopted standard combining AC and DC charging in a single connector.

   - Application: Prominent in Europe and increasingly embraced by automakers globally.

2. CHAdeMO:

   - Overview: A fast-charging standard developed by Japanese companies, supporting DC charging.

- Application: Commonly found in Japanese and European electric vehicles.

3. Tesla Supercharger:

- Overview: Proprietary to Tesla, providing high-speed DC charging for Tesla vehicles.

- Application: Exclusive to Tesla vehicles, with Supercharger stations strategically located worldwide.

Understanding Interoperability and Seamless Charging:

1. Universal Compatibility: Charging standards ensure that electric vehicles (EVs) from different manufacturers can charge at any charging station adhering to the same standard. This universal compatibility fosters a seamless charging experience for EV users.

2. Public Charging Network Integration: Charging stations worldwide conforming to common standards contribute to the establishment of comprehensive public charging networks. EV users can confidently navigate diverse regions, knowing that charging infrastructure adheres to recognized standards.

3. Simplified User Experience: Standards create a plug-and-charge environment, streamlining the user experience. EV drivers can connect to charging stations without compatibility concerns, fostering widespread adoption.

Evolution of Standards to Accommodate Technological Advancements:

1. Increased Charging Speeds: As technological advancements drive higher charging speeds, standards evolve to support these advancements. New iterations of standards accommodate faster charging rates, reducing overall charging times.

2. Bidirectional Charging and V2G Integration: Future standards are exploring bidirectional charging, allowing vehicles to not only consume energy but also feed surplus energy back to the grid (Vehicle-to-Grid or V2G). This evolution aligns with the broader trend of smart grids and energy management.

3. Global Collaboration and Standardization Bodies: Organizations like the International Electrotechnical Commission (IEC) and regional standardization bodies facilitate global collaboration. Their efforts lead to the development and refinement of charging standards, ensuring a cohesive and evolving framework.

In the dynamic landscape of EV charging, charging standards act as the guiding principles that harmonize the diverse array of electric vehicles and charging infrastructure. As standards continue to evolve, they propel the electric mobility revolution forward, ensuring a future where seamless charging is a universal expectation.

Smart Charging Solutions: Navigating the Future of EV Power

What is Smart Charging?

Smart charging refers to an intelligent and connected approach to electric vehicle (EV) charging, leveraging technology to optimize the charging process. This entails using data, communication, and advanced control systems to enhance the efficiency, reliability, and sustainability of EV charging infrastructure.

Why is Smart Charging Important?

1. Energy Optimization:

- Dynamic Load Management: Smart charging systems can dynamically manage the load on the grid, optimizing charging times based on energy demand and availability. This ensures efficient use of energy resources.

2. Cost Savings:

- Time-of-Use Rates: Smart charging enables users to take advantage of time-of-use electricity rates. By scheduling charging during off-peak hours when electricity costs are lower, users can achieve cost savings.

3. Grid Stability and Demand Response:

- Grid Integration: Smart charging solutions contribute to grid stability by managing the flow of electricity. They can also participate in demand response programs, adjusting charging rates based on grid conditions.

4. Enhanced User Experience:

- Connectivity and Remote Control: Users can remotely monitor and control their EV charging sessions through mobile apps or online platforms. This connectivity enhances the overall user experience, providing convenience and flexibility.

5. Electricity from Renewable Sources:

- Integration with Renewables: Smart charging can be integrated with renewable energy sources, allowing users to prioritize charging when renewable energy generation is high. This supports a more sustainable and eco-friendly charging process.

6. Vehicle-to-Grid (V2G) Capability:

- Bidirectional Charging: Some smart charging solutions support bidirectional charging, enabling vehicles to not only consume electricity but also send excess energy back to the grid. This Vehicle-to-Grid (V2G) capability enhances grid resilience and offers potential revenue streams for EV owners.

7. Load Balancing in Urban Areas:

- Distribution of Charging Loads: In urban environments with high concentrations of EVs, smart charging can distribute charging loads across different stations, preventing localized grid congestion.

8. Integration with IoT and AI:

- Advanced Technologies: Integration with the Internet of Things (IoT) and Artificial Intelligence (AI) allows for predictive analytics, learning user behaviors, and adapting charging schedules based on individual preferences and patterns.

Smart charging solutions are pivotal in advancing the electric mobility ecosystem. By harnessing technology and connectivity, these solutions not only make EV charging more efficient and cost-effective but also contribute to a smarter, more resilient, and sustainable energy future.

The Concept of Smart Charging: Transforming EV Power Dynamics

Defining Smart Charging in the Context of Electric Vehicles:

Smart charging is a visionary approach to electric vehicle (EV) charging, where technology and intelligence converge to optimize the charging process. It goes beyond traditional charging methods, introducing dynamic and adaptive strategies to enhance efficiency, grid resilience, and user experience.

1. Adaptive Charging Schedules:

- Smart charging systems analyze factors such as energy demand, grid conditions, and user preferences to dynamically adjust charging schedules.

- Users can benefit from optimized charging times, cost savings, and reduced impact on the electricity grid.

2. Connectivity and Control:

- Leveraging connectivity, smart charging allows users to remotely monitor and control their EV charging sessions through mobile apps or online platforms.

- This connectivity enhances user convenience, providing real-time insights and enabling on-the-go adjustments.

3. Grid Integration:

- Smart charging solutions integrate with the smart grid, enabling bidirectional communication between the EV, charging infrastructure, and the electricity grid.

- This integration facilitates load management, grid balancing, and the ability to respond to demand fluctuations.

Integration with the Smart Grid and Renewable Energy Sources:

1. Dynamic Load Management:

- Smart charging interfaces with the smart grid to adapt charging rates based on grid conditions and demand. This dynamic load management ensures optimal use of available electricity resources.

2. Time-of-Use Optimization:

- Integration with time-of-use rates enables smart charging systems to schedule charging during periods of lower electricity costs.

- Users can take advantage of off-peak rates, promoting cost savings and supporting grid stability.

3. Renewable Energy Prioritization:

- Smart charging can be designed to prioritize charging when renewable energy sources, such as solar or wind power, are abundant.

- This aligns with sustainability goals, minimizing the carbon footprint associated with EV charging.

4. Vehicle-to-Grid (V2G) Capability:

- Some smart charging systems support bidirectional charging, allowing EVs to send excess energy back to the grid.

- Vehicle-to-Grid (V2G) capability enhances grid resilience, supports renewable energy integration, and offers potential revenue streams for EV owners.

5. Predictive Analytics and AI:

- Integration with the Internet of Things (IoT) and Artificial Intelligence (AI) enables predictive analytics.

- Smart charging systems can learn user behaviors, adapt to patterns, and optimize charging schedules for individual preferences.

The concept of smart charging transcends traditional charging paradigms, ushering in a new era where electric vehicles become integral components of a dynamic, intelligent, and sustainable energy ecosystem. As technology continues to evolve, smart charging will play a central role in shaping the future of electric mobility and its harmonious integration with the broader energy landscape.

Benefits of Smart Charging: Transforming the EV Charging Landscape

1. Energy Optimization and Cost Savings:

- Dynamic Charging Schedules: Smart charging systems analyze energy demand, grid conditions, and time-of-use rates to dynamically optimize charging schedules.

- Cost-Effective Charging: By scheduling charging during periods of lower electricity costs, users can achieve cost savings and contribute to efficient energy use.

2. Demand Response Capabilities for Grid Stability:

- Grid Integration: Smart charging solutions contribute to grid stability by responding to real-time grid conditions.

- Load Management: These systems can adjust charging rates or delay charging during peak demand periods, supporting grid reliability and preventing congestion.

3. Enhanced User Experience Through Connectivity:

- Remote Monitoring and Control: Users can remotely monitor and control their charging sessions through mobile apps or online platforms.

- Real-Time Insights: Connectivity provides real-time insights into charging status, allowing users to make informed decisions and adjustments on the go.

4. Integration with Renewable Energy Sources:

- Renewable Energy Prioritization: Smart charging can prioritize charging when renewable energy generation is high, aligning with sustainability goals.

- Reduced Environmental Impact: By integrating with renewables, smart charging minimizes the carbon footprint associated with EV charging.

5. Vehicle-to-Grid (V2G) Capability:

- Bidirectional Charging: Some smart charging systems support bidirectional charging, enabling EVs to send excess energy back to the grid.

- Grid Resilience: Vehicle-to-Grid (V2G) capability enhances grid resilience by allowing EVs to act as distributed energy resources.

6. Predictive Analytics and Data Analytics:

- Learning User Behavior: Integration with the Internet of Things (IoT) and Artificial Intelligence (AI) enables predictive analytics.

- Adaptive Charging: Smart charging systems can learn user behaviors over time, adapting charging schedules to individual preferences.

7. Balancing Load in Urban Areas:

- Distributed Charging Loads: In urban environments with high concentrations of EVs, smart charging can distribute charging loads across different stations, preventing localized grid congestion.

Smart charging emerges as a catalyst for transforming the EV charging experience. By combining energy optimization, grid responsiveness, enhanced user connectivity, and sustainable practices, smart charging not only meets the needs of individual EV users but also contributes to the resilience and efficiency of the broader energy infrastructure.

Technological Innovations in Smart Charging: Paving the Way for Tomorrow's EV Ecosystem

Introduction to Emerging Technologies in Smart Charging:

1. Internet of Things (IoT) Integration:

- Connected Charging Infrastructure: Smart charging systems leverage IoT devices to connect and communicate with charging stations, enabling seamless data exchange and control.

2. Artificial Intelligence (AI) for Predictive Analytics:

- Learning User Behavior: AI algorithms analyze user charging patterns, adapting charging schedules to individual preferences and predicting future charging needs.

- Optimizing Energy Use: Predictive analytics help optimize energy consumption, ensuring efficient use of available resources.

3. Blockchain for Secure Transactions:

- Secure and Transparent Transactions: Blockchain technology enhances the security and transparency of transactions within smart charging networks, ensuring trust and reliability.

Vehicle-to-Grid (V2G) Capabilities and Bidirectional Charging:

1. Vehicle-to-Grid (V2G) Technology:

- Bi-Directional Energy Flow: V2G enables bidirectional energy flow between EVs and the grid.

- Grid Support: EVs equipped with V2G capabilities can provide services to the grid, such as load balancing, peak shaving, and grid stabilization.

2. Bidirectional Charging:

- Energy Exchange with the Grid: Bidirectional charging allows EVs to not only receive energy from the grid but also feed surplus energy back.

- Grid Resilience: This capability enhances grid resilience by turning EVs into flexible energy assets that can respond to grid demand and fluctuations.

3. Advanced Battery Management Systems:

- Optimizing Battery Health: Smart charging systems incorporate advanced Battery Management Systems (BMS) to optimize charging rates and ensure the health of EV batteries.

- Extended Battery Lifespan: Adaptive charging based on battery conditions helps extend the lifespan of EV batteries.

4. Wireless Charging Technology:

- Effortless Charging Experience: Wireless charging eliminates the need for physical cables, providing a seamless and convenient charging experience for EV users.

- Integration with Smart Charging: Wireless charging can be integrated into smart charging networks, adding another layer of flexibility and user convenience.

5. Grid-Interactive Vehicles:

- Real-time Grid Communication: Grid-interactive vehicles can communicate in real-time with the grid, adjusting their charging behavior based on grid conditions.

- Grid-Aware Charging: This technology ensures that EVs contribute to grid stability and efficiency.

Technological innovations in smart charging are propelling the electric vehicle ecosystem toward greater efficiency, sustainability, and grid integration. By harnessing the power of IoT, AI, blockchain, and bidirectional charging capabilities, the future of smart charging promises a more dynamic and intelligent approach to electric mobility.

CHAPTER 03

MARKET TRENDS AND OPPORTUNITIES

Global EV Market Growth: Transforming the Automotive Horizon

Introduction:

In recent years, the global electric vehicle (EV) market has undergone a profound metamorphosis, reshaping the automotive landscape and fundamentally altering the way we envision the future of transportation. This chapter unravels the compelling narrative of the rapid ascent of the global EV market, a journey characterized by shifts in consumer preferences, groundbreaking technological advancements, and an unwavering commitment to environmental sustainability.

Key Elements:

1. Consumer Preferences:

- Explore how consumers are increasingly embracing electric vehicles as viable alternatives to traditional internal combustion engine vehicles.

- Understand the factors influencing this shift, including the appeal of cleaner, more sustainable transportation options and the expanding range of available EV models.

2. Technological Advancements:

- Delve into the dynamic realm of technological breakthroughs propelling the EV market forward.

- Uncover advancements in battery technology, electric drivetrains, and vehicle connectivity that are not only enhancing the performance of electric vehicles but also reshaping the overall automotive industry.

3. Environmental Considerations:

- Examine the growing awareness and concern for environmental sustainability, driving individuals, corporations, and governments towards cleaner transportation solutions.

- Understand how the global focus on reducing carbon emissions and mitigating climate change has become a pivotal catalyst for the proliferation of electric vehicles.

Global Impact:

The surge in global EV market growth is not confined to a specific region but resonates on a global scale. As countries around the world align their policies, industries, and infrastructures with the electric mobility revolution, the market growth becomes a testament to the collective pursuit of a more sustainable and eco-friendly future.

Conclusion:

This chapter sets the stage for a comprehensive exploration of the multifaceted dynamics fueling the global rise of electric vehicles. From evolving consumer preferences to groundbreaking technological innovations and the overarching commitment to environmental well-being, the narrative of global EV market growth reflects a paradigm shift towards a cleaner, more sustainable era of transportation.

Surge in Adoption: The Global Embrace of Electric Vehicles
Exploring Significant Growth:

The surge in adoption of electric vehicles (EVs) marks a pivotal moment in the evolution of transportation worldwide. This section delves into the remarkable growth, capturing the essence of how EVs are increasingly becoming the preferred choice for consumers across diverse regions.

Key Elements:

1. Global Momentum:

   - Witness the widespread adoption of electric vehicles on a global scale, transcending geographical boundaries.

   - Understand the factors contributing to this momentum, ranging from environmental consciousness to advancements in EV technology.

2. Expanding Model Range:

   - Explore the diverse landscape of electric vehicles, with an expanding range of models spanning various vehicle segments.

   - Witness the evolution from compact electric cars to electric SUVs, crossovers, and even electric commercial vehicles, showcasing the versatility and broad appeal of EVs.

3. Consumer Preferences Redefined:

   - Examine how consumer preferences are undergoing a paradigm shift, with more individuals opting for electric vehicles as their primary mode of transportation.

   - Understand the motivations driving this change, including the desire for reduced environmental impact, lower operating costs, and the allure of cutting-edge electric vehicle technology.

4. Innovations in Mobility:

   - Witness the transformative impact of electric vehicles on the overall mobility landscape.

- Explore how the surge in EV adoption is influencing not only personal transportation but also contributing to the reimagining of public transportation and shared mobility solutions.

Across Vehicle Segments:

The surge in adoption is not confined to a specific vehicle segment but permeates diverse categories. From compact electric cars that cater to urban commuting to electric SUVs providing versatility for families, the adoption trend spans the entire spectrum of vehicle types.

Conclusion:

The surge in adoption underscores a pivotal shift in how the world perceives and embraces transportation. As electric vehicles become increasingly accessible, diverse, and integrated into the fabric of daily life, the global momentum reflects a transformative journey towards a sustainable and electrified future of mobility.

Regional Dynamics: Unveiling Variations in EV Market Growth

Exploring Regional Variations:

Understanding the landscape of electric vehicle (EV) market growth requires a nuanced examination of regional dynamics. This section navigates through the diverse contexts, shedding light on leading markets, emerging players, and the unique factors shaping the trajectory of electric mobility in different parts of the world.

Key Elements:

1. Leading Markets:

- Examine regions that have emerged as pioneers in driving EV adoption.

- Uncover insights into the factors contributing to the leadership of certain markets, including supportive government policies, robust charging infrastructure, and high levels of environmental consciousness.

2. Emerging Players:

- Identify regions that are witnessing a burgeoning interest and rising prominence in the electric vehicle space.

- Understand the catalysts propelling these emerging players, encompassing government initiatives, technological innovation, and changing consumer preferences.

3. Government Policies and Incentives:

- Explore how regional governments are influencing the EV landscape through policies, incentives, and regulatory frameworks.

- Understand the impact of financial incentives, tax credits, and emission regulations on EV adoption in different regions.

4. Charging Infrastructure Development:

- Analyze the state of charging infrastructure in various regions, recognizing the critical role it plays in facilitating widespread EV adoption.

- Uncover trends in the deployment of charging networks, including advancements in fast-charging capabilities and the integration of smart charging solutions.

Examples of Regional Dynamics:

1. Europe:

- Leading the charge with ambitious emissions targets, Europe has become a stronghold for electric vehicles. Countries like Norway, the Netherlands, and Germany are at the forefront, supported by robust charging networks and favorable government policies.

2. Asia-Pacific:

- Emerging as a powerhouse in the EV landscape, countries in the Asia-Pacific region, including China and South Korea, are witnessing substantial growth. These nations are driven by technological advancements, strong government support, and a rapidly expanding market.

3. North America:

- With a mix of established players and new entrants, North America showcases a dynamic EV market. The United States, in particular, is experiencing significant growth driven by consumer demand, regulatory measures, and a growing charging infrastructure.

Conclusion:

Regional dynamics in the electric vehicle market highlight the diverse approaches, challenges, and opportunities that define the global landscape. As leading markets pave the way and emerging players contribute to the electrification momentum, understanding these regional variations is integral to envisioning the future of electric mobility on a worldwide scale.

Market Drivers: Propelling the Global Surge in EV Demand
Identifying Key Drivers:

The surge in global electric vehicle (EV) demand is propelled by a synergy of influential factors that span environmental consciousness, regulatory support, and breakthroughs in battery technology. This section unveils the drivers steering the unprecedented growth in the adoption of electric vehicles.

Key Drivers:

1. Environmental Awareness:

- Shifting Perspectives: A heightened awareness of environmental concerns, including climate change and air quality, is prompting individuals and societies to seek sustainable transportation alternatives.

- Reducing Carbon Footprint: Consumers are increasingly opting for electric vehicles as a means to reduce their carbon footprint and contribute to a cleaner, greener future.

2. Regulatory Support:

- Emission Reduction Targets: Governments worldwide are setting ambitious emission reduction targets, necessitating a transition to cleaner transportation solutions.

- Incentive Programs: Financial incentives, tax credits, and regulatory frameworks that favor electric vehicles are driving consumer adoption and encouraging automakers to invest in electric mobility.

3. Advancements in Battery Technology:

- Enhanced Range and Performance: Ongoing advancements in battery technology are extending the range and improving the performance of electric vehicles, addressing one of the key concerns of consumers.

- Declining Costs: The evolution of battery technology is contributing to cost reductions, making electric vehicles more economically viable and competitive with traditional vehicles.

4. Government Initiatives:

- Charging Infrastructure Investment: Governments are actively investing in the development of EV charging infrastructure to alleviate range anxiety and facilitate widespread adoption.

- Research and Development Funding: Government funding for research and development in electric vehicle technology is fostering innovation, leading to breakthroughs in efficiency and sustainability.

5. Consumer Incentives:

- Financial Support: Various governments offer direct financial incentives, including subsidies and rebates, to encourage consumers to choose electric vehicles.

- Access to HOV Lanes: Additional perks, such as access to high-occupancy vehicle (HOV) lanes, further incentivize consumers to opt for electric vehicles.

6. Advocacy and Public Awareness:

- Influential Advocacy: The efforts of environmental organizations, celebrities, and influencers advocating for electric mobility are raising public awareness and influencing consumer choices.

- Educational Campaigns: Educational campaigns highlighting the benefits of electric vehicles and dispelling myths contribute to changing perceptions and fostering acceptance.

Conclusion:

The collaborative impact of environmental awareness, regulatory support, advancements in battery technology, government initiatives, consumer incentives, and influential advocacy collectively fuels the global surge in electric vehicle demand. As these drivers continue to evolve, they shape the trajectory of the electric mobility revolution, guiding the world toward a sustainable and electrified future of transportation.

Government Incentives and Regulations: Catalysts of Electric Vehicle Adoption
Introduction:

In the realm of electric mobility, the role of government policies is paramount, steering the course of adoption and influencing the dynamics of the electric vehicle (EV) market. This chapter delves into the intricate landscape of government incentives and regulations, unraveling their significance in propelling the widespread adoption of electric vehicles.

Key Elements:

1. Policy Landscape:

- Governments worldwide are actively formulating policies to accelerate the transition to electric vehicles, recognizing their pivotal role in mitigating environmental impact and reducing dependence on fossil fuels.

2. Financial Incentives:

- Financial incentives, including tax credits, rebates, and subsidies, are instrumental in incentivizing consumers to embrace electric vehicles.

- These incentives aim to make EVs more economically appealing, bridging the cost gap and encouraging a shift towards sustainable transportation.

3. Regulatory Framework:

- Regulatory measures, such as emission standards and zero-emission vehicle (ZEV) mandates, set the stage for automakers to prioritize and invest in electric vehicle technologies.

- These regulations align with environmental goals, driving the industry towards cleaner and more sustainable practices.

4. Charging Infrastructure Investment:

- Governments play a crucial role in the development of charging infrastructure, addressing range anxiety and facilitating the growth of electric vehicles.

- Investment in charging networks enhances the accessibility and convenience of EVs, contributing to their widespread adoption.

Importance:

1. Accelerating Adoption:

- Government incentives and regulations serve as accelerators, spurring the uptake of electric vehicles among consumers and businesses.

- Financial incentives lower barriers to entry, making EVs more accessible to a broader demographic.

2. Environmental Impact:

- Regulatory frameworks promote the reduction of emissions and encourage the adoption of cleaner transportation alternatives.

- The combined effect of these regulations contributes to a substantial decrease in the overall environmental impact of the transportation sector.

3. Industry Transformation:

- Policies shape the automotive industry by steering investments, research, and development towards electric vehicle technologies.

- Incentives drive innovation, fostering a competitive landscape and encouraging automakers to prioritize sustainable practices.

4. Infrastructure Development:

- Government investment in charging infrastructure addresses a critical hurdle in EV adoption—range anxiety.

- A well-developed charging network ensures that consumers have convenient access to charging stations, facilitating the seamless integration of electric vehicles into daily life.

Conclusion:

Government incentives and regulations emerge as pivotal forces propelling the electric vehicle revolution. As nations align their policies with sustainability goals, the significance of these measures becomes instrumental in shaping a future where electric mobility is not just a choice but a cornerstone of global transportation.

Financial Incentives: Energizing Electric Vehicle Adoption

Analyzing Government Support:

Financial incentives stand as a cornerstone in the concerted efforts of governments worldwide to energize the adoption of electric vehicles (EVs). This section delves into the multifaceted landscape of government subsidies, tax credits, and other financial incentives designed to encourage individuals and businesses to embrace the electric mobility revolution.

Key Components:

1. Subsidies for Purchase:

   - Governments often offer direct subsidies to individuals upon the purchase of electric vehicles.

   - These subsidies aim to reduce the upfront cost of EVs, making them more economically competitive with traditional internal combustion engine vehicles.

2. Tax Credits:

   - Tax credits serve as a powerful financial incentive, allowing individuals to offset a portion of their tax liability based on the purchase of an electric vehicle.

   - This approach provides indirect financial support, encouraging individuals to consider the long-term economic benefits of owning an electric vehicle.

3. Rebates and Vouchers:

   - Rebate programs offer post-purchase financial incentives, providing consumers with a refund or voucher after buying an electric vehicle.

- Such programs contribute to the overall affordability of electric vehicles and act as a reward for choosing a sustainable transportation option.

4. Reduced Registration Fees:

- Some jurisdictions opt to reduce or waive registration fees for electric vehicles.

- This not only provides financial relief for EV owners but also aligns with the goal of incentivizing cleaner modes of transportation.

5. Incentives for Fleet Purchases:

- Governments may extend financial incentives to businesses and organizations making bulk purchases of electric vehicles for their fleets.

- This approach aims to accelerate the electrification of commercial transportation and reduce the overall carbon footprint of fleets.

Importance:

1. Affordability and Accessibility:

- Financial incentives directly contribute to making electric vehicles more affordable for a broader range of consumers.

- By addressing cost concerns, governments seek to increase the accessibility of EVs, fostering a more inclusive transition to electric mobility.

2. Economic Considerations:

- Tax credits and other financial benefits create economic incentives for individuals, aligning the decision to adopt an electric vehicle with potential long-term financial savings.

- These incentives showcase the government's commitment to supporting sustainable choices.

3. Market Stimulation:

- Financial incentives stimulate demand in the electric vehicle market, driving sales and encouraging automakers to invest in and expand their electric vehicle offerings.

- The resulting market growth contributes to the overall transition to cleaner transportation.

4. Environmental Impact:

- As more individuals choose electric vehicles due to financial incentives, the cumulative reduction in emissions and environmental impact becomes significant.

- Financial incentives thus play a vital role in achieving broader environmental goals.

Conclusion:

Financial incentives serve as a catalyst, injecting momentum into the global shift towards electric mobility. As governments strategically employ subsidies, tax credits, and other financial tools, they not only make electric vehicles more attractive on a personal and economic level but also advance the collective journey towards a sustainable and cleaner transportation future.

Regulatory Framework: Guiding Electric Mobility through Standards and Mandates
Exploring Regulatory Measures:

The regulatory framework is a vital instrument wielded by governments to guide the trajectory of electric mobility. This section delves into the intricate web of regulatory measures, encompassing emission standards, zero-emission vehicle (ZEV) mandates, and restrictions on internal combustion engine (ICE) vehicles, all designed to shape a cleaner and more sustainable future of transportation.

Key Components:

1. Emission Standards:

  - Governments globally are implementing stringent emission standards to curb the environmental impact of the transportation sector.

  - Emission standards for vehicles, including those related to carbon dioxide (CO_2) and other pollutants, push automakers to develop and produce cleaner, more fuel-efficient vehicles.

2. Zero-Emission Vehicle Mandates:

  - Zero-emission vehicle mandates require automakers to produce and sell a certain percentage of vehicles with zero tailpipe emissions.

- These mandates act as a powerful catalyst for the development and adoption of electric vehicles, compelling automakers to invest in and prioritize clean transportation solutions.

3. Restrictions on Internal Combustion Engine Vehicles:

- Some regions are imposing restrictions on the sale of new internal combustion engine vehicles within a specified timeframe.

- These restrictions signal a transition towards fully electrified transportation, encouraging automakers to accelerate their shift away from traditional fossil fuel-based vehicles.

4. Incentives for EV Adoption:

- Conversely, governments may offer incentives to consumers for adopting electric vehicles, aligning with regulatory goals to reduce emissions.

- These incentives may include financial rewards, preferential parking, or access to high-occupancy vehicle (HOV) lanes, creating a supportive environment for electric vehicle adoption.

5. Charging Infrastructure Requirements:

- Regulatory frameworks often include requirements for the development and expansion of electric vehicle charging infrastructure.

- Mandates related to charging infrastructure ensure that the necessary facilities are in place to support the growing number of electric vehicles on the road.

Importance:

1. Environmental Impact Mitigation:

- Emission standards and ZEV mandates directly contribute to mitigating the environmental impact of the transportation sector, reducing air pollution and greenhouse gas emissions.

2. Market Transformation:

- By enforcing regulations, governments guide the transformation of the automotive market towards cleaner and more sustainable alternatives.

- These regulations drive automakers to innovate and invest in electric vehicle technologies.

3. Consumer Confidence:

- Regulatory frameworks provide a clear signal to consumers about the commitment to electric mobility, instilling confidence in the long-term viability and support for electric vehicles.

4. Accelerating Transition:

- Restrictions on internal combustion engine vehicles and incentives for EV adoption accelerate the transition to electric mobility, aligning with broader sustainability goals.

Conclusion:

The regulatory framework emerges as a pivotal tool in steering the course of electric mobility. By setting standards, mandates, and incentives, governments actively contribute to a future where transportation is not only efficient and convenient but also environmentally sustainable.

Infrastructure Investment: Powering the Electric Vehicle Ecosystem
Examining Government Initiatives:

Infrastructure investment, particularly in charging networks, stands as a linchpin in the strategic efforts of governments to foster the growth of the electric vehicle (EV) ecosystem. This section delves into the significance of government initiatives focused on developing charging infrastructure and creating an environment conducive to the seamless integration of electric vehicles.

Key Components:

1. Charging Network Expansion:

   - Governments are actively investing in the expansion of charging networks to address range anxiety and provide a reliable and extensive charging infrastructure for EV owners.

   - The deployment of charging stations in strategic locations, including highways, urban areas, and public spaces, ensures accessibility and convenience for electric vehicle users.

2. Fast-Charging Technologies:

- Infrastructure investment includes the incorporation of fast-charging technologies to reduce charging times significantly.

- Fast-charging stations, strategically placed along major routes, enable long-distance travel and enhance the practicality of electric vehicles for a broader range of users.

3. Public-Private Partnerships:

- Governments often engage in partnerships with private entities to accelerate the development of charging infrastructure.

- Public-private collaborations leverage the strengths of both sectors, combining governmental support with private innovation and efficiency.

4. Smart Charging Solutions:

- Investment in smart charging solutions introduces intelligence into the charging infrastructure, optimizing energy usage, and enhancing user experience.

- Smart solutions may include real-time data monitoring, remote management, and integration with renewable energy sources, contributing to a more sustainable and efficient charging network.

Importance:

1. Overcoming Range Anxiety:

   - A well-developed charging infrastructure alleviates range anxiety, a common concern among prospective EV owners.

   - Users gain confidence in the availability of charging stations, enabling them to plan longer journeys without the fear of running out of power.

2. Accelerating EV Adoption:

   - Accessible and efficient charging infrastructure accelerates the adoption of electric vehicles by addressing one of the key barriers to entry.

   - A robust charging network encourages more individuals to choose electric vehicles as a practical and viable transportation option.

3. Supporting Diverse Charging Needs:

   - Infrastructure investment caters to diverse charging needs, including home charging, workplace charging, and public charging, ensuring that EV users have versatile and convenient charging options.

4. Boosting Economic Growth:

   - Investment in charging infrastructure stimulates economic growth by creating jobs, fostering innovation in the energy sector, and attracting investments in the burgeoning electric mobility industry.

5. Environmental Sustainability:

- By facilitating the transition to electric vehicles, infrastructure investment contributes to environmental sustainability by reducing reliance on traditional fossil fuels and lowering overall emissions.

Conclusion:

Infrastructure investment emerges as a pivotal catalyst, shaping the landscape of electric mobility. As governments prioritize the development of charging networks and embrace innovative solutions, they not only enhance the user experience but also pave the way for a future where electric vehicles are seamlessly integrated into the fabric of daily life.

Business Opportunities in the EV Charging Industry: Navigating the Electric Avenue

Introduction:

As the electric vehicle (EV) market charges ahead, a myriad of business opportunities unfolds within the EV charging industry. This section illuminates the dynamic landscape of possibilities, offering insights into the diverse avenues for entrepreneurs, investors, and innovators to carve their niche in this transformative sector.

Key Elements:

1. Charging Infrastructure Investment:

- Entrepreneurs can tap into the growing demand for charging infrastructure by investing in the development of charging stations.

- Opportunities abound for public charging networks, workplace charging solutions, and residential charging infrastructure.

2. Technology and Software Solutions:

- The integration of smart charging solutions opens avenues for entrepreneurs to develop and provide cutting-edge software solutions.

- Innovations in billing systems, remote monitoring, and data analytics contribute to the efficiency and intelligence of EV charging networks.

3. Partnerships and Collaborations:

- Collaboration is a strategic move for businesses looking to thrive in the EV charging industry.

- Partnerships between automakers, energy companies, and technology firms can lead to synergies that drive innovation and expand the reach of charging networks.

4. EV Service Providers:

- Entrepreneurs can explore opportunities in ancillary services related to electric vehicles, including maintenance, battery swapping, and fleet management.

- Emerging business models within the EV service sector offer a diverse range of opportunities for entrepreneurial ventures.

Importance:

1. Meeting Growing Demand:

- As the number of electric vehicles on the road increases, the demand for charging infrastructure grows exponentially.

- Entrepreneurs who invest in meeting this demand play a crucial role in supporting the widespread adoption of electric vehicles.

2. Driving Technological Innovation:

- Businesses focusing on technology and software solutions contribute to the continuous evolution of the EV charging industry.

- Innovations in user experience, connectivity, and data analytics enhance the efficiency and appeal of EV charging networks.

3. Addressing Unique Challenges:

- Entrepreneurs have the opportunity to address specific challenges within the EV ecosystem, such as developing solutions for charging in dense urban areas or creating seamless interoperability between different charging networks.

4. Supporting Sustainable Transportation:

- Business opportunities within the EV charging industry align with the broader goal of supporting sustainable transportation.

- Entrepreneurs contributing to the growth of electric mobility actively participate in creating a cleaner and more environmentally friendly future.

Conclusion:

The burgeoning EV market not only presents challenges but also a wealth of opportunities for those willing to navigate the electric avenue. Entrepreneurs and businesses that strategically position themselves within the EV charging industry contribute to shaping the future of transportation while unlocking new realms of innovation and economic growth.

Charging Infrastructure Investment: Powering the Future of Electric Mobility
Exploring Business Opportunities:

Charging infrastructure investment represents a pivotal avenue for businesses to play a transformative role in the electric vehicle (EV) ecosystem. This section delves into the multifaceted opportunities within the realm of investing in and developing EV charging infrastructure, encompassing public charging stations, workplace solutions, and residential charging.

Key Opportunities:

1. Public Charging Networks:

- Urban and Highway Charging Hubs: Entrepreneurs can seize opportunities in establishing public charging hubs strategically located in urban areas and along highways.

- Fast-Charging Stations: Investment in fast-charging stations enables businesses to cater to the needs of EV owners seeking rapid charging options, especially during long-distance travel.

2. Workplace Charging Solutions:

- Corporate Partnerships: Businesses can collaborate with corporations to install workplace charging stations, contributing to employee satisfaction and promoting sustainable commuting.

- Fleet Charging Services: Entrepreneurs can explore fleet charging solutions, catering to businesses with electric vehicle fleets by providing efficient and cost-effective charging infrastructure.

3. Residential Charging Infrastructure:

- Home Charging Solutions: Investing in home charging solutions, including residential charging stations and installation services, addresses the needs of EV owners who prefer the convenience of charging at home.

- Community Charging Initiatives: Entrepreneurs can explore opportunities in developing community-based charging solutions, such as shared residential charging stations for neighborhoods or apartment complexes.

4. Smart Charging Technologies:

- Billing and Payment Systems: Entrepreneurs can innovate in developing efficient billing and payment systems for charging services, streamlining the financial transactions within the EV charging ecosystem.

- Data Analytics: Investment in data analytics solutions enhances the intelligence of charging infrastructure, providing insights into user behavior, usage patterns, and system performance.

Importance:

1. Meeting Growing Demand:

- Investing in charging infrastructure meets the escalating demand for convenient and accessible charging solutions as the number of electric vehicles on the road continues to rise.

2. Enhancing User Experience:

- Well-designed and strategically located charging infrastructure enhances the overall user experience, addressing concerns related to range anxiety and contributing to the increased adoption of electric vehicles.

3. Supporting Urban Planning:

- Businesses investing in charging infrastructure play a crucial role in supporting urban planning initiatives focused on sustainable transportation, contributing to cleaner and more livable cities.

4. Enabling Fleets and Businesses:

   - Charging infrastructure investments that cater to the needs of electric vehicle fleets and corporate entities contribute to the electrification of businesses, promoting a more sustainable and environmentally conscious approach to transportation.

   Conclusion:

   Charging infrastructure investment stands at the forefront of shaping the electric mobility landscape. Businesses that strategically invest in and develop EV charging infrastructure not only support the current wave of electric vehicle adoption but also lay the foundation for a future where charging is seamless, accessible, and an integral part of everyday life.
   Technology and Software Solutions: Energizing the Intelligence of EV Charging

   Exploring Innovations:

   In the dynamic realm of electric vehicle (EV) charging, technology and software solutions stand as pillars of innovation. This section navigates through the significance of these advancements, ranging from smart charging platforms to sophisticated billing and payment systems.

   Key Innovations:

   1. Smart Charging Platforms:

   - Real-Time Monitoring: Smart charging platforms enable real-time monitoring of charging stations, providing operators and users with insights into usage patterns, energy consumption, and station availability.

- Remote Management: The ability to remotely manage and control charging stations enhances operational efficiency, allowing for updates, maintenance, and troubleshooting without physical intervention.

2. Billing and Payment Systems:

- Efficient Transaction Processing: Innovations in billing and payment systems streamline the financial transactions associated with EV charging services, creating a seamless and user-friendly experience.

- Subscription Models: Some platforms explore subscription-based models, offering users a convenient and cost-effective way to access charging services with simplified payment structures.

3. Data Analytics and Insights:

- User Behavior Analysis: Advanced data analytics solutions delve into user behavior, providing valuable insights into charging preferences, peak usage times, and overall trends.

- Predictive Maintenance: Predictive analytics can anticipate maintenance needs, reducing downtime for charging stations and enhancing their overall reliability.

4. Connectivity and Interoperability:

- Interconnected Networks: Innovations focus on enhancing connectivity and interoperability among different charging networks, ensuring a seamless experience for EV owners regardless of the charging station provider.

- Roaming Agreements: Platforms facilitating roaming agreements enable users to access multiple charging networks with a single account, promoting convenience and flexibility.

Importance:

1. Enhancing User Experience:

- Technology and software solutions play a pivotal role in enhancing the overall user experience, making EV charging more convenient, accessible, and user-friendly.

- Real-time information and remote management contribute to a smoother and more efficient charging process.

2. Operational Efficiency:

- Smart charging platforms and sophisticated billing systems enhance the operational efficiency of charging networks.

- Remote management capabilities and predictive maintenance contribute to reducing downtime and improving the reliability of charging infrastructure.

3. Supporting Sustainable Practices:

- Data analytics solutions contribute to sustainable practices by optimizing charging station usage, reducing energy waste, and supporting grid management efforts.

- Connectivity and interoperability foster a collaborative ecosystem that promotes the widespread adoption of electric vehicles.

4. Future-Proofing Infrastructure:

- Investing in technology and software solutions future-proofs charging infrastructure, allowing for adaptability to emerging technologies, evolving user preferences, and industry standards.

- Connectivity and interoperability ensure that charging infrastructure remains relevant and accessible as the electric mobility landscape evolves.

Conclusion:

Innovations in technology and software solutions are at the core of shaping the future of EV charging. As these advancements continue to evolve, they not only contribute to the efficiency and intelligence of charging infrastructure but also play a crucial role in fostering a sustainable and interconnected electric mobility ecosystem.

Partnerships and Collaborations: Driving Synergies in the EV Charging Ecosystem

Exploring Collaborative Opportunities:

Partnerships and collaborations are instrumental in creating synergies within the electric vehicle (EV) charging ecosystem. This section illuminates the potential for collaborative efforts between automakers, energy companies, and tech firms, fostering innovation and advancing the integration of EVs into the broader energy landscape.

Key Collaborative Opportunities:

1. Automaker-Utility Alliances:

- Integrated Charging Solutions: Collaborations between automakers and utility companies can lead to integrated charging solutions, where electric vehicles seamlessly connect with the energy grid for optimized charging and energy management.

- Exclusive Charging Benefits: Automaker-utility alliances can offer exclusive charging benefits for customers, enhancing the overall ownership experience and incentivizing EV adoption.

2. Energy Companies and Charging Infrastructure Providers:

- Renewable Energy Integration: Partnerships between energy companies and charging infrastructure providers can facilitate the integration of renewable energy sources into charging networks, promoting sustainable and clean energy practices.

- Grid Management Solutions: Collaborations may focus on developing grid management solutions to optimize the distribution of energy for EV charging, ensuring efficient utilization of resources.

3. Tech Firm-Automaker Collaborations:

- Connectivity and Interoperability: Tech firms and automakers can collaborate to enhance connectivity and interoperability between electric vehicles and charging networks.

- Innovative User Interfaces: Collaborative efforts can result in the development of innovative user interfaces and applications that simplify the charging experience and provide valuable insights to users.

4. Joint Research and Development Initiatives:

- Battery Technology Advancements: Collaborations between automakers, energy companies, and tech firms can fuel joint research and development initiatives, focusing on advancements in battery technology for improved range, efficiency, and sustainability.

- Emerging Technologies: Partnerships can explore emerging technologies such as wireless charging, bidirectional charging, and autonomous charging solutions, pushing the boundaries of innovation in the EV charging landscape.

Importance:

1. Cross-Industry Synergies:

- Partnerships between automakers, energy companies, and tech firms create cross-industry synergies, leveraging the strengths of each sector to drive innovation and efficiency within the EV charging ecosystem.

2. Comprehensive User Solutions:

- Collaborative efforts enable the development of comprehensive solutions that address the entire spectrum of user needs, from vehicle charging and energy management to connectivity and user interfaces.

3. Grid Optimization and Sustainability:

- Collaborations contribute to grid optimization by aligning EV charging with renewable energy sources and developing solutions for efficient energy distribution.

- These efforts actively support sustainability goals, making the transition to electric mobility more environmentally friendly.

4. Market Expansion and Accessibility:

- Partnerships expand the reach and accessibility of charging networks, making electric vehicles more practical for a broader range of users.

- Joint initiatives can lead to the deployment of charging infrastructure in previously underserved areas, contributing to the overall growth of the EV market.

Conclusion:

Partnerships and collaborations stand as linchpins in propelling the electric vehicle charging ecosystem forward. As diverse industries unite to innovate and address challenges collaboratively, the result is a more connected, sustainable, and user-centric electric mobility landscape.

EV Service Providers: Pioneering Business Models in Electric Mobility
Exploring Emerging Business Models:

EV service providers play a pivotal role in shaping the electric mobility landscape. This section illuminates the diverse business models emerging within this sector, encompassing maintenance services, battery swapping solutions, and innovative fleet management approaches.

Key Business Models:

1. Maintenance Services:

- Specialized EV Maintenance Centers: Companies focusing on maintenance services establish specialized centers equipped to handle the unique needs of electric vehicles, including battery diagnostics, software updates, and general upkeep.

- Mobile Maintenance Units: Innovative models involve mobile maintenance units that offer on-site services, providing convenience for EV owners who may not have easy access to service centers.

2. Battery Swapping Solutions:

- Quick and Efficient Swapping Stations: EV service providers explore battery swapping as a solution for addressing range anxiety. Stations equipped for rapid battery swaps enable drivers to replace depleted batteries with fully charged ones, minimizing downtime.

- Subscription-Based Swapping Plans: Some providers offer subscription-based plans for battery swapping, allowing users to access the service without the upfront cost of battery ownership.

3. Fleet Management Services:

- Comprehensive Fleet Electrification: Companies specializing in fleet management services work with businesses to transition their vehicle fleets to electric. This includes strategic planning, charging infrastructure implementation, and ongoing fleet maintenance.

- Telematics and Efficiency Optimization: Innovative fleet management models incorporate telematics and data analytics to optimize the efficiency of electric vehicle fleets. This includes route optimization, predictive maintenance, and real-time monitoring.

4. Charging Network Integration:

- Partnerships for Charging Access: Some service providers collaborate with existing charging networks to offer seamless access for their customers. This ensures that EV owners under their services can easily find and utilize charging infrastructure.

- Exclusive Charging Benefits: Service providers may negotiate exclusive charging benefits with charging networks, providing added value to their customer base.

Importance:

1. User-Centric Support:

- EV service providers focus on offering user-centric support, addressing the unique needs of electric vehicle owners, and providing specialized services tailored to the intricacies of electric mobility.

2. Overcoming Adoption Barriers:

- Business models centered around maintenance, battery swapping, and fleet management contribute to overcoming barriers to EV adoption, such as range anxiety and concerns about maintenance costs.

3. Enabling Fleet Electrification:

- Fleet management services actively support the electrification of commercial fleets, contributing to a reduction in overall emissions and promoting sustainability within the business sector.

4. Enhancing Accessibility:

- By offering innovative solutions like mobile maintenance units and battery swapping, service providers enhance the accessibility of electric vehicle ownership, making it more practical for a broader audience.

Conclusion:

EV service providers exemplify the adaptability and innovation required in the electric mobility era. As they pioneer business models focused on user support, fleet electrification, and seamless charging experiences, these providers play a crucial role in advancing the widespread adoption of electric vehicles.

CHAPTER 04

PLANNING YOUR EV CHARGING BUSINESS

The First Step: Defining Your Vision and Objectives

Embarking on the journey to plan your EV charging business begins with a clear vision and well-defined objectives. Establishing your goals and aspirations for the business lays the foundation for strategic planning and decision-making.

Importance of Planning:

1. Strategic Direction:

- Planning provides a roadmap, guiding the business toward specific objectives and milestones.
- A well-defined vision sets the strategic direction, helping you make informed decisions aligned with your long-term goals.

2. Resource Allocation:
- Planning assists in efficient resource allocation, ensuring that budget, infrastructure, and efforts are directed toward areas that contribute most significantly to the business's success.

3. Risk Mitigation:
- A thorough planning process allows for the identification and mitigation of potential risks and challenges.
- By anticipating obstacles, you can develop strategies to overcome them and enhance the resilience of your business.

4. Market Alignment:
- Planning helps align your business with market trends, user needs, and regulatory landscapes.
- Understanding the market ensures that your EV charging business remains relevant and responsive to evolving industry dynamics.

5. Financial Viability:
- Detailed planning, including budgeting and financial analysis, is crucial for ensuring the financial viability of your business.
- It aids in identifying potential revenue streams, estimating costs, and conducting a realistic assessment of return on investment.

6. Stakeholder Alignment:

- Clearly defined objectives facilitate alignment with stakeholders, including potential investors, partners, and local authorities.
- Effective communication of your business vision enhances collaboration and support from key stakeholders.

7. Adaptability and Innovation:
- Planning allows for adaptability and innovation as the business landscape evolves.
- By being proactive and flexible, you can incorporate emerging technologies and trends, ensuring your EV charging business remains at the forefront of industry advancements.

Conclusion:
The first step in planning your EV charging business, defining your vision and objectives, sets the stage for a well-organized and purposeful venture. The importance of planning cannot be overstated—it serves as a compass, guiding your business toward sustainable growth, resilience, and success in the dynamic landscape of electric mobility.

Strategic Placement: Powering the Reach of EV Charging Stations

Significance:

1. High-Traffic Areas:
- Visibility and Accessibility: Placing EV charging stations in high-traffic areas enhances visibility and accessibility for users.
- Capture Urban Commuters: Urban hubs, shopping centers, and popular destinations become ideal locations,

capturing the attention of commuters and increasing station utilization.

2. Proximity to Highways:
- Enabling Long-Distance Travel: Stations near highways facilitate long-distance travel, addressing range anxiety and promoting the feasibility of electric vehicles for inter-city journeys.
- Strategic Pit Stops: Highway-adjacent charging stations serve as strategic pit stops, encouraging EV owners to recharge during travels.

3. Urban and Suburban Accessibility:
- Residential Convenience: Including charging stations in residential areas caters to the convenience of EV owners who prefer charging close to home.
- Workplace Charging: Strategic placement includes workplace charging solutions, supporting users who charge their vehicles while at work.

4. Collaborative Partnerships:
- Business Collaborations: Collaborating with businesses, municipalities, and property owners enables strategic placement in areas with high footfall.
- Public-Private Initiatives: Public-private initiatives can leverage existing infrastructure, such as parking lots, to optimize placement and maximize accessibility.

Considerations:

1. User Behavior Patterns:
- Analyzing Charging Needs: Understanding user behavior patterns helps identify optimal locations based on charging needs.

- Customized Solutions: Different users may prefer different charging locations, and strategic placement aims to provide a variety of options.

2. Accessibility for All Users:
- Inclusive Placement: Ensuring accessibility for both urban and suburban users promote inclusivity in the adoption of electric vehicles.
- Addressing Range Anxiety: Strategically placed stations contribute to overcoming range anxiety, making EVs more practical for a diverse user base.

3. Public Perception:
- Visibility and Trust: Strategically placed charging stations contribute to the visibility of electric mobility, fostering public trust and interest.
- Integration with Urban Landscape: Integration into the urban and suburban landscape ensures that charging stations become an integral part of daily life.

4. Scalability and Expansion:
- Scalable Network: Strategic placement considers scalability, allowing for the expansion of the charging network as the demand for EV charging grows.
- Flexible Placement Models: Adaptable placement models enable adjustments based on user behavior, changing demographics, and evolving city planning.

Conclusion:
Strategic placement of EV charging stations is a critical component in the success of an electric vehicle charging business. By considering factors such as high-traffic areas, highway proximity, and accessibility for various user demographics, businesses can create a network that not only

meets user needs but also actively contributes to the widespread adoption of electric mobility.

Understanding User Behavior: A Cornerstone of EV Charging Success

Analyzing Charging Needs:

1. Optimal Location Identification:
   - Tailoring to User Preferences: Analyzing user behavior patterns allows for the identification of optimal charging locations tailored to user preferences.
   - Data-Driven Decision-Making: Data on charging frequency, preferred times, and duration aids in making informed decisions about station placement.

2. Residential Charging Considerations:
   - Convenience for Daily Commutes: Recognizing the importance of residential charging addresses the convenience factor for users who prefer to charge at home for their daily commutes.
   - Nighttime Charging Patterns: Understanding that residential users may prefer nighttime charging influences the availability and accessibility of charging stations in these areas.

3. Workplace Charging Solutions:
   - Supporting Daily Work Routines: Workplace charging addresses the needs of users who spend significant time at work, integrating charging into their daily routines.
   - Extended Charging Durations: Recognizing that workplace charging may involve longer charging durations allows for the provision of facilities conducive to longer stays.

4. Public Charging Network Optimization:
   - Balancing Commuter and Travel Needs: Comprehensive understanding of user behavior balances the

needs of commuters requiring quick top-ups and travelers seeking longer charging sessions.
- Strategic Placement in High-Traffic Areas: Strategic placement in high-traffic public areas caters to diverse user needs, ensuring the charging network serves a broad demographic.

Creating a Comprehensive Charging Network:

1. Inclusivity and Accessibility:
- Broad User Demographics: A deep understanding of user behavior ensures that charging stations cater to a broad range of demographics, making electric vehicles accessible to a wider audience.
- Addressing Range Anxiety: By strategically placing charging stations where users naturally spend time, such as shopping centers or entertainment venues, the network addresses range anxiety and promotes confidence in EV adoption.

2. Balancing Peak Usage Times:
- Optimizing Charging Infrastructure: Understanding peak usage times helps optimize charging infrastructure, ensuring that stations are available during high-demand periods.
- User-Centric Scheduling: Considering user behavior patterns aids in developing user-centric scheduling strategies to manage congestion and enhance the overall charging experience.

3. Data-Driven Expansion:
- Scalable Network Growth: Utilizing user behavior data supports scalable network growth, allowing for expansion based on demand trends.

- Adaptive Planning: Adaptive planning based on user behavior ensures that the charging network evolves in tandem with changing user preferences and urban development.

Conclusion:
Understanding user behavior is paramount in creating a successful and user-friendly EV charging network. By analyzing charging needs, considering residential, workplace, and public charging dynamics, and leveraging data-driven insights, businesses can tailor their infrastructure to meet the diverse requirements of electric vehicle users, fostering a seamless and inclusive charging experience.

Collaborative Partnerships: Powering the Growth of EV Charging Infrastructure

Defining Collaborative Partnerships:

1. Strategic Alliances:
- Business Collaborations: Collaborating with businesses creates strategic alliances that benefit both parties. Businesses can attract environmentally conscious customers, while charging infrastructure providers gain access to high-traffic locations.

2. Municipal Engagement:
- City Integration: Partnerships with municipalities integrate charging infrastructure into city planning, contributing to the city's sustainability goals.
- Urban Development Initiatives: Municipalities may incentivize the deployment of charging stations as part of broader urban development initiatives.

3. Property Owner Collaboration:

- Leveraging Existing Infrastructure: Collaborating with property owners allows for the utilization of existing infrastructure, such as parking lots or commercial spaces, for charging stations.

- Mutual Benefits: Property owners benefit from increased foot traffic, and charging infrastructure providers secure prime locations.

Importance of Collaborative Partnerships:

1. Prime Location Access:
- Unlocking High-Traffic Areas: Collaborative partnerships provide access to prime locations in collaboration with businesses, municipalities, and property owners.

- Maximizing Visibility: Charging stations placed in collaboration with established entities maximize visibility and accessibility, driving usage.

2. Community Integration:
- Building Community Support: Partnerships with municipalities foster community support for EV adoption, making charging infrastructure an integrated part of the community.

- Navigating Regulatory Landscape: Municipal collaborations help navigate local regulations, ensuring compliance and smooth deployment.

3. Enhanced User Experience:
- Convenience for Users: Strategic placement in collaboration with businesses and property owners enhances the overall user experience by providing convenient charging options.

- Diverse Charging Environments: Charging stations in varied locations, from shopping centers to corporate offices, cater to diverse user preferences.

4. Cost-Effective Deployment:
- Optimizing Infrastructure Costs: Collaborative partnerships can optimize infrastructure costs by leveraging existing facilities and spaces.
- Shared Investment: Businesses and property owners may contribute to the investment, making the deployment more cost-effective for charging infrastructure providers.

5. Promoting Sustainable Practices:
- Aligning with Municipal Goals: Collaborating with municipalities aligns charging infrastructure deployment with broader city goals for sustainability and environmental responsibility.
- Educational Initiatives: Partnerships create opportunities for educational initiatives, fostering awareness and understanding of electric mobility within the community.

6. Network Scalability:
- Agile Expansion: Collaborative partnerships facilitate agile expansion as businesses, municipalities, and property owners become stakeholders in the success of the charging network.
- Adapting to Growth Trends: The collaborative model allows for adaptation to changing trends in user behavior, ensuring that the network evolves in sync with demand.

Conclusion:
Collaborative partnerships play a pivotal role in securing prime locations for charging infrastructure,

enhancing user experience, and promoting sustainable electric mobility practices. By leveraging these partnerships, businesses can strategically deploy charging stations, contributing to the growth and accessibility of electric vehicle charging networks.

Infrastructure Requirements for EV Charging Stations

Understanding the Vital Components:

1. Charging Stations:
   - Level 1 Charging: Basic household charging stations suitable for overnight charging at residential locations.
   - Level 2 Charging: More powerful chargers suitable for both residential and public locations, offering faster charging than Level 1.
   - DC Fast Chargers: High-speed chargers designed for quick charging, particularly suitable for long-distance travel and high-traffic areas.

2. Power Supply:
   - Adequate Electrical Capacity: Ensuring the availability of sufficient electrical capacity to support the charging stations.
   - Compatibility with Charger Types: Aligning power supply with the requirements of Level 1, Level 2, or DC fast chargers deployed.

3. Technology Integration:
   - Smart Charging Solutions: Incorporating smart charging technologies for efficient management of charging stations.

- Connectivity Features: Ensuring connectivity features for user-friendly experiences, such as mobile apps, payment solutions, and real-time status updates.

4. Charging Connectors and Standards:
- Compatibility: Adopting standard charging connectors to ensure compatibility with a wide range of electric vehicles.
- Adherence to Global Standards: Aligning with global charging standards to facilitate interoperability and convenience for users.

Location-Specific Considerations:

1. Residential Charging Infrastructure:
- Home Charging Stations: Providing Level 1 or Level 2 charging stations for residential use.
- Electrical Panel Upgrades: Ensuring that residential electrical panels can support the additional load from EV charging.

2. Workplace Charging Solutions:
- Charging Stations in Parking Lots: Installing charging stations in workplace parking lots for employee use.
- Integration with Corporate Infrastructure: Coordinating with facility management to seamlessly integrate charging infrastructure with corporate facilities.

3. Public Charging Network:
- High-Traffic Locations: Strategically placing charging stations in high-traffic areas such as shopping centers, restaurants, and entertainment venues.
- Urban and Suburban Integration: Ensuring a mix of urban and suburban charging stations to address diverse user needs.

4. DC Fast Charging Stations:
- High-Speed Charging Hubs: Deploying DC fast chargers in high-traffic hubs for quick and convenient charging.
- Long-Distance Travel Routes: Placing DC fast chargers along highways and major routes to support long-distance travel.

Regulatory Compliance and Safety:

1. Safety Measures:
- Compliance with Safety Standards: Adhering to safety standards and regulations to ensure the secure operation of charging stations.
- Emergency Protocols: Implementing emergency protocols and safety features to address unforeseen situations.

2. Accessibility and Inclusivity:
- ADA Compliance: Ensuring accessibility for users with disabilities, including compliance with the Americans with Disabilities Act (ADA).
- Inclusive Design: Incorporating design elements that cater to a diverse range of users and vehicle types.

Conclusion:
Infrastructure requirements for EV charging stations encompass a comprehensive set of components, from the types of chargers to technology integration and location-specific considerations. Meeting these requirements ensures the successful deployment and operation of an effective and user-friendly electric vehicle charging network.

Charging Station Types: Tailoring Solutions for Diverse User Needs

1. Level 1 Charging:
   - Location Suitability:
   - Residential: Ideal for home charging, allowing users to plug their vehicles into standard household outlets.
   - User Needs:
   - Daily Commuting: Suited for users with shorter daily commutes who can charge their vehicles overnight.
   - Convenience: Provides a convenient option for residential charging without requiring dedicated charging infrastructure.

2. Level 2 Charging:
   - Location Suitability:
   - Residential: Suitable for home use with dedicated Level 2 charging stations.
   - Workplace: Ideal for workplace charging in parking lots or dedicated charging areas.
   - Public Spaces: Deployed in public spaces such as shopping centers, restaurants, and urban areas.
   - User Needs:
   - Daily Commuting: Faster charging for users with longer daily commutes, enabling convenient charging at home or work.
   - Extended Stops: Ideal for users making longer stops in public spaces, offering a balance between charging speed and accessibility.

3. DC Fast Chargers:
   - Location Suitability:
   - High-Traffic Areas: Deployed in high-traffic locations, including highways, major travel routes, and urban hubs.

- Long-Distance Travel Routes: Positioned along highways to support long-distance travel.
- User Needs:
- Quick Charging: Designed for users in need of rapid charging, reducing wait times during extended journeys.
- Urban Convenience: Suited for urban environments where users may have limited time for charging but need a quick top-up.

Considerations for Different Locations:

1. Residential Areas:
- Level 1 and Level 2: Residential areas benefit from Level 1 and Level 2 chargers, supporting overnight charging for residents and employees.
- Community Charging Hubs: Public spaces within residential areas can host Level 2 chargers, creating community charging hubs.

2. Workplace Charging:
- Level 2: Workplace charging is often facilitated by Level 2 stations in dedicated parking lots.
- Employee Convenience: Enables employees to charge their vehicles during work hours, supporting the adoption of electric vehicles.

3. Public Spaces:
- Mixed Deployment: Public spaces, including shopping centers and entertainment venues, may feature a mix of Level 2 and DC fast chargers.
- Variety for Users: Providing various charging options caters to different user needs, from quick top-ups to extended charging sessions.

4. Highway and Travel Routes:
- DC Fast Chargers: Highways and travel routes predominantly feature DC fast chargers.
- Long-Distance Travel Support: Essential for EV users embarking on long-distance journeys, providing quick charging for extended travel.

User-Focused Flexibility:

1. Daily Commuters:
- Level 1 or Level 2: Suited for daily commuters with predictable charging patterns who can utilize Level 1 or Level 2 charging at home or work.

2. Urban Dwellers:
- Level 2 or DC Fast Chargers: Urban users benefit from the flexibility of both Level 2 chargers in public spaces and quick-charging options for on-the-go convenience.

3. Long-Distance Travelers:
- DC Fast Chargers: Essential for users engaged in long-distance travel, providing rapid charging at strategically located stations along major routes.

Conclusion:
Understanding the distinct characteristics of Level 1, Level 2, and DC fast chargers allows for strategic deployment, meeting the diverse needs of users across residential, workplace, and public locations. A well-balanced mix of these charging station types contributes to the accessibility and widespread adoption of electric vehicles.

Power Supply Considerations: Empowering the Charging Network

Ensuring Adequate Electrical Capacity:

1. Charging Station Functionality:
   - Importance:
   - Optimal Performance: Assessing power supply ensures that charging stations operate optimally, delivering the intended charging speed.
   - User Experience: Adequate electrical capacity prevents underperformance, enhancing the overall user experience by minimizing wait times.

2. Compatibility with Charger Types:
   - Importance:
   - Aligning with Charger Specifications: Different charging station types (Level 1, Level 2, DC fast chargers) have varied power requirements.
   - Avoiding Overloads: Ensuring compatibility prevents overloads, safeguarding both the charging infrastructure and the electrical grid.

Tailoring to Location-Specific Needs:

1. Residential Charging Infrastructure:
   - Importance:
   - Home Charging Considerations: Assessing power supply at residential locations is crucial for supporting Level 1 and Level 2 charging.
   - Capacity for Multiple Users: Ensuring capacity supports multiple charging stations in residential areas where multiple users may simultaneously charge their vehicles.

2. Workplace Charging Solutions:
   - Importance:

- Supporting Employee Charging: Adequate power supply at workplaces accommodates multiple employees charging their vehicles during work hours.
- Enhancing Corporate Sustainability: Workplace charging aligns with corporate sustainability goals, necessitating a robust power supply infrastructure.

3. Public Charging Network:
  - Importance:
- High-Traffic Locations: High-traffic public spaces hosting Level 2 and DC fast chargers require substantial power supply.
- Meeting Peak Demands: Power supply considerations address peak usage times, ensuring stations operate efficiently during periods of high demand.

4. DC Fast Charging Stations:
  - Importance:
- Rapid Charging Demands: DC fast chargers have higher power requirements to facilitate quick charging.
- Preventing Bottlenecks: Adequate power supply prevents bottlenecks, allowing DC fast chargers to operate at their full capacity.

Planning for Future Growth:

1. Scalability:
  - Importance:
- Accommodating Growth: Assessing power supply for scalability enables the charging network to expand in response to increasing demand.
- Adapting to EV Adoption Trends: Proactive planning ensures the power supply can meet the growing needs of an expanding electric vehicle market.

Regulatory Compliance and Safety:

1. Safety Measures:
   - Importance:
   - Preventing Overloads: Ensuring sufficient power supply prevents overloads, reducing the risk of electrical failures or safety hazards.
   - Regulatory Compliance: Adhering to safety standards and regulatory requirements mitigates risks associated with inadequate power supply.

Conclusion:
Power supply considerations are fundamental to the successful operation of charging stations. Addressing these considerations not only ensures optimal functionality and user satisfaction but also supports the scalability and safety of the electric vehicle charging infrastructure. Adequate power supply is the linchpin in building a robust and reliable charging network that can meet the diverse needs of users and adapt to the evolving landscape of electric mobility.

Technology Integration: Elevating Efficiency and User Experience in Charging Infrastructure

1. Smart Charging Solutions:
   - Efficiency Enhancement:
   - Dynamic Load Management: Smart charging systems optimize energy distribution, preventing grid overloads during peak periods.
   - Energy Cost Optimization: Integration of real-time energy pricing allows users to charge when rates are lower, optimizing cost-efficiency.

2. Connectivity Features:

- User Experience Improvement:
    - Mobile Apps: Integration with mobile apps provides users with real-time charging station status, reservation capabilities, and payment options, enhancing convenience.
    - Real-Time Updates: Users receive notifications about charging completion, enabling efficient vehicle retrieval and minimizing wait times.

3. Payment Solutions:
    - Convenience and Accessibility:
    - Contactless Payments: Integration with contactless payment options streamlines the charging process, ensuring quick and secure transactions.
    - Subscription Models: Offering subscription-based payment models provides users with flexibility and cost predictability.

4. Energy Management Systems:
    - Grid Interaction:
    - Bi-Directional Charging: Advanced systems allow for bidirectional charging, enabling energy flow from vehicles back to the grid during peak demand, supporting grid stability.
    - Load Balancing: Smart systems distribute the load across charging stations intelligently, preventing local grid congestion.

5. Charging Connectors and Standards:
    - Interoperability and Compatibility:
    - Global Standards Compliance: Integrating with global charging standards ensures interoperability, allowing users to connect their vehicles to various charging stations seamlessly.

- Future-Proofing: Adherence to evolving standards supports the compatibility of the charging infrastructure with new electric vehicle models.

6. Data Analytics:
  - Operational Optimization:
  - Usage Patterns Analysis: Analyzing data on user behavior and station usage helps optimize charging station placement and operational schedules.
  - Predictive Maintenance: Data analytics enable predictive maintenance, reducing downtime and ensuring stations remain operational.

7. Cybersecurity Measures:
  - Security Enhancement:
  - Secure Transactions: Implementing robust cybersecurity measures ensures the security of user transactions and personal data.
  - Protection against Cyber Threats: Integration of security protocols safeguards the charging infrastructure against cyber threats, ensuring uninterrupted service.

8. V2G (Vehicle-to-Grid) Integration:
  - Grid Support and Sustainability:
  - Grid Stability Enhancement: V2G integration allows electric vehicles to feed energy back to the grid during peak demand, contributing to grid stability.
  - Sustainability Features: Encouraging V2G adoption aligns with sustainability goals, showcasing the charging infrastructure's commitment to environmental responsibility.

Benefits of Technology Integration:

1. User Convenience:
    - Seamless Experience: Technology integration ensures a seamless and user-friendly charging experience, from finding available stations to making payments.

2. Efficient Resource Utilization:
    - Grid Optimization: Smart charging systems optimize energy distribution, preventing grid overloads and contributing to overall grid efficiency.

3. Adaptability to Future Trends:
    - Future-Proof Infrastructure: Integrating with evolving technologies ensures that the charging infrastructure remains relevant and adaptable to future industry developments.

4. Operational Efficiency:
    - Data-Driven Decision-Making: Data analytics and smart features contribute to operational efficiency, allowing for informed decision-making and proactive maintenance.

5. Sustainability and Grid Support:
    - V2G Contributions: Integration with V2G supports sustainability goals, leveraging electric vehicles as contributors to grid stability and renewable energy utilization.

Conclusion:
Technology integration in charging infrastructure enhances operational efficiency, user experience, and sustainability. As smart charging solutions continue to evolve, integrating these technologies ensures that the charging network remains at the forefront of innovation, providing users with convenient, efficient, and environmentally responsible electric vehicle charging solutions.

Budgeting and Financing in EV Charging Business: Ensuring Viability and Growth

1. Budgeting:
   - Strategic Planning:
     - Resource Allocation: Budgeting involves strategically allocating resources, including funds, for various aspects of the EV charging business, such as infrastructure deployment, maintenance, and marketing.
     - Risk Mitigation: Comprehensive budgeting helps identify potential risks and uncertainties, allowing for proactive measures to mitigate financial challenges.

2. Financial Planning:
   - Long-Term Viability:
     - Profitability Analysis: Financial planning assesses the business's profitability, considering revenue streams, operational costs, and potential return on investment.
     - Sustainability Measures: It involves planning for sustainable financial practices to ensure the long-term viability and growth of the EV charging business.

3. Infrastructure Investment:
   - Capital Allocation:
     - Charging Station Deployment: Budgeting directs funds toward the deployment of charging infrastructure, including Level 1, Level 2, and DC fast chargers, catering to diverse user needs.
     - Technology Integration: Allocating funds for integrating smart technologies ensures the deployment of efficient and user-friendly charging solutions.

4. Operational Expenses:
   - Maintenance and Upkeep:

- Regular Maintenance: Budgeting covers regular maintenance costs to ensure the reliability and functionality of charging stations.
- Upgrades and Innovations: Provision for upgrades and innovations helps the business stay competitive and adapt to evolving industry standards.

5. Marketing and Promotion:
- Market Visibility:
- Brand Promotion: Allocating funds for marketing efforts enhances brand visibility, attracting users to the charging network.
- Community Engagement: Budgeting for community engagement initiatives fosters positive relationships, contributing to user trust and loyalty.

6. Regulatory Compliance:
- Legal and Compliance Costs:
- Adherence to Standards: Budgeting includes provisions for legal and compliance costs associated with adhering to industry standards, safety regulations, and environmental guidelines.
- Risk Management: Financial planning considers potential legal challenges and allocates resources for risk management measures.

7. Employee Training and Support:
- Human Resources Investment:
- Training Programs: Allocating funds for employee training ensures that staff members are well-equipped to handle various aspects of the charging infrastructure, including customer support and technical maintenance.
- Workforce Development: Budgeting for workforce development contributes to employee satisfaction

and skill enhancement, positively impacting the quality of service.

8. Contingency Funds:
   - Risk Mitigation:
   - Unexpected Expenses: Maintaining contingency funds in the budget allows the business to address unexpected expenses, ensuring operational continuity during unforeseen circumstances.
   - Adapting to Market Changes: Budgeting for contingencies helps the business adapt to market changes and seize emerging opportunities.

Financing:
   - Capital Procurement:
   - Investor Partnerships: Seeking financing through investor partnerships or venture capital enables the business to secure the necessary capital for infrastructure development and expansion.
   - Government Grants and Incentives: Exploring government grants and incentives for electric vehicle charging businesses provides financial support and promotes sustainable practices.

2. Loan Structures:
   - Debt Financing:
   - Bank Loans: Securing loans from financial institutions offers an avenue for debt financing, allowing the business to access capital for growth and development.
   - Interest Rates and Repayment Plans: Evaluating interest rates and establishing favorable repayment plans are crucial aspects of financing through loans.

3. Public-Private Partnerships:

- Collaborative Funding Models:
    - Government Collaboration: Public-private partnerships involve collaboration with government entities to secure funding for charging infrastructure development.
    - Private Sector Contributions: Engaging with private sector partners for joint funding initiatives helps diversify financial sources.

4. Revenue Models:
    - Sustainable Income Streams:
    - User Fees: Developing sustainable revenue models, such as user fees or subscription plans, ensures a steady income stream for the ongoing operation and maintenance of charging stations.
    - Partnership Revenues: Exploring partnerships with businesses for charging station deployment can generate additional revenues through collaborative funding or revenue-sharing models.

5. Grant Applications:
    - Government and Industry Grants:
    - Grant Opportunities: Actively seeking and applying for government and industry grants for EV charging businesses provides financial support, especially for projects aligned with environmental and sustainability goals.
    - Compliance with Grant Requirements: Ensuring budget alignment with grant requirements enhances the likelihood of successful grant applications.

Importance of Budgeting and Financing:

1. Financial Stability:
    - Risk Mitigation: Proper budgeting and financing strategies mitigate financial risks, ensuring the business's stability and resilience in the face of challenges.

2. Strategic Growth:
- Infrastructure Expansion: Adequate financing supports the strategic expansion of the charging infrastructure, enabling the business to meet growing demand and explore new market opportunities.

3. Operational Efficiency:
- Maintenance and Upgrades: Budgeting for regular maintenance and upgrades contributes to the operational efficiency and reliability of the charging network.

4. Competitive Edge:
- Marketing Initiatives: Financing marketing initiatives helps create a competitive edge by enhancing brand visibility and attracting a larger user base.

5. Sustainability:
- Environmental Commitment: Budgeting for sustainable practices and adhering to environmentally friendly standards aligns the business with sustainability goals.

6. User Satisfaction:
- Service Quality: Adequate budgeting for employee training and support contributes to high service quality, enhancing user satisfaction and loyalty.

Conclusion:
Budgeting and financing are integral components of establishing and maintaining a successful EV charging business. They ensure financial stability, strategic growth, operational efficiency, and the ability to adapt to market changes, contributing to the long-term viability and success of the charging infrastructure.

Financing Options for EV Charging Business: Fostering Sustainable Growth

1. Government Grants and Subsidies:
   - Overview:
   - Financial Support: Government grants provide direct financial support for the deployment and operation of EV charging infrastructure.
   - Environmental Initiatives: Many grants are aligned with environmental goals, encouraging businesses to adopt sustainable practices.

2. Public-Private Partnerships (PPPs):
   - Collaborative Funding:
   - Joint Initiatives: Collaborating with government entities or private investors in PPPs allows shared funding for charging infrastructure projects.
   - Risk Sharing: Partnerships distribute financial risks among involved entities, promoting shared responsibility for project success.

3. Private Investments:
   - Investor Partnerships:
   - Venture Capital: Seeking investments from venture capitalists provides capital for infrastructure development and operational expansion.
   - Private Equity: Private equity funding offers opportunities for businesses to secure capital in exchange for a stake in the company.

4. Bank Loans and Financial Institutions:
   - Debt Financing:
   - Bank Loans: Traditional bank loans provide businesses with a source of debt financing, enabling them to access capital for charging network development.

- Interest Rates and Terms: Evaluating interest rates, repayment terms, and collateral requirements is essential when considering loans from financial institutions.

5. Revenue-Sharing Models:
 - Partnership Revenues:
 - Collaborative Agreements: Establishing revenue-sharing agreements with partners or businesses allows for shared income from charging stations.
 - Business Collaborations: Partnering with businesses for charging station deployment and sharing revenues creates mutually beneficial financial arrangements.

6. User Fees and Subscription Models:
 - Direct User Contributions:
 - Pay-Per-Use: Charging station operators can generate revenue directly from users by implementing pay-per-use models.
 - Subscription Plans: Offering subscription plans provides users with regular access to charging services in exchange for a recurring fee.

7. Carbon Credits and Environmental Initiatives:
 - Environmental Revenue Streams:
 - Carbon Credits: Participating in carbon credit programs allows businesses to generate revenue by contributing to carbon reduction efforts.
 - Environmental Certifications: Earning certifications for sustainable practices may open avenues for financial incentives or partnerships.

8. Manufacturer and Industry Support:
 - Corporate Collaboration:

- Support from Automakers: Collaboration with automakers may involve financial support for charging infrastructure development, especially when aligned with specific vehicle models.
- Industry Associations: Participating in industry associations may provide access to collective funding efforts or support from established players in the electric vehicle sector.

9. Community Fundraising and Crowdfunding:
   - Local Engagement:
   - Community Support: Engaging with local communities through fundraising initiatives or crowdfunding campaigns can generate financial support from residents and businesses.
   - Building Local Relationships: Community involvement fosters a sense of ownership and support for the charging infrastructure, contributing to long-term success.

Considerations When Exploring Financing Options:

1. Alignment with Business Goals:
   - Strategic Objectives: Choosing financing options that align with the business's strategic objectives ensures a cohesive approach to growth and sustainability.

2. Regulatory Compliance:
   - Grant Requirements: Ensuring compliance with grant and subsidy requirements is crucial for securing government funding and maintaining eligibility for incentives.

3. Risk Management:
   - Financial Stability: Assessing the risks associated with each financing option allows businesses to make

informed decisions and implement effective risk management strategies.

4. Long-Term Viability:
- Sustainability Measures: Considering the long-term sustainability of financing options ensures ongoing support for the growth and maintenance of the charging network.

5. Diversification:
- Balanced Funding Sources: Diversifying funding sources helps mitigate financial risks and dependencies on a single financing method.

6. Local Engagement:
- Community Relationships: Community-focused financing options, such as crowdfunding, contribute to building strong local relationships and support for the charging infrastructure.

Conclusion:
Exploring a mix of financing options is essential for the successful development and operation of an EV charging business. By strategically combining government grants, private investments, partnerships, and innovative revenue models, businesses can secure the necessary capital to build a robust and sustainable charging network. Each financing option brings its unique advantages, and a well-balanced approach ensures financial resilience and long-term success.
Return on Investment (ROI) Analysis for EV Charging Business: Navigating Financial Success

1. Importance of ROI Analysis:
- Strategic Decision-Making:

- Informed Choices: ROI analysis provides critical insights that guide strategic decisions in infrastructure deployment, technology integration, and business expansion.
- Resource Allocation: It aids in allocating resources effectively by identifying areas that contribute most significantly to financial success.

2. Revenue Streams Evaluation:
- Diverse Income Sources:
- User Fees: Analyzing potential revenue from user fees helps gauge the financial viability of different charging models.
- Partnership Revenues: Assessing income from partnerships and collaborations provides a comprehensive view of revenue streams.

3. User Projections:
- Forecasting Growth:
- User Adoption Rates: Projections on user adoption rates assist in estimating the number of users and their impact on revenue.
- Regional Variations: Considering regional variations in user behavior helps tailor charging network strategies to specific markets.

4. Operational Costs Assessment:
- Comprehensive Analysis:
- Maintenance and Upkeep: Evaluating ongoing operational costs, including maintenance and upgrades, ensures accurate financial planning.
- Employee Training: Factoring in costs for employee training contributes to a skilled and efficient workforce, positively impacting service quality.

5. Technology Integration Impact:

- Costs vs. Benefits:
- Initial Investments: Weighing the initial costs of technology integration against long-term benefits ensures a balanced approach to innovation.
- Efficiency Gains: Assessing how technology enhances operational efficiency and user experience contributes to ROI calculations.

6. Community Engagement:
- Local Impact:
- Community Fundraising: ROI analysis considers the impact of community engagement initiatives, such as crowdfunding, on the overall financial success of the charging network.
- Long-Term Support: Building strong local relationships through engagement initiatives contributes to sustained community support, influencing ROI positively.

7. Regulatory Compliance and Incentives:
- Financial Implications:
- Grant Requirements: Ensuring compliance with grant and incentive program requirements is crucial for leveraging financial support without compromising ROI.
- Environmental Certifications: Earning environmental certifications may open avenues for additional incentives, impacting ROI positively.

8. Risk Mitigation:
- Financial Stability:
- Contingency Planning: Identifying potential risks and incorporating contingency plans in the ROI analysis ensures financial stability during unforeseen circumstances.

- Adapting to Market Changes: Proactively assessing market risks helps the business adapt to changes, minimizing negative impacts on ROI.

9. Long-Term Viability:
  - Sustainable Practices:
    - Environmental Considerations: ROI analysis incorporates the long-term benefits of sustainable practices, aligning with environmental goals and ensuring the business's viability over time.
    - Scalability: Evaluating scalability based on projected growth and market trends contributes to long-term financial success.

ROI Analysis as a Dynamic Process:
  - Continuous Monitoring:
    - Adaptation to Changes: ROI analysis is an ongoing process that adapts to market changes, technology advancements, and shifts in user behavior.
    - Optimization Opportunities: Continuously monitoring ROI provides opportunities for optimization, ensuring the business remains financially competitive.

Conclusion:
Conducting a thorough ROI analysis is indispensable for the success of an EV charging business. By assessing revenue streams, user projections, operational costs, and the impact of various factors on financial performance, businesses can make informed decisions, allocate resources effectively, and navigate the evolving landscape of the electric vehicle charging industry with financial acumen.

Long-Term Sustainability in EV Charging Business: Nurturing Financial Viability and Adaptability

1. Strategic Planning for Growth:
   - Market Trends Analysis:
   - Anticipation of Trends: Continuously analyze market trends, including advancements in electric vehicle technology and user preferences, to strategically position the business for sustained growth.
   - Scalability Considerations: Evaluate scalability options, considering potential increases in user demand and the expansion of electric vehicle models.

2. Technology Integration for Future-Proofing:
   - Adopting Innovative Solutions:
   - Continuous Innovation: Embrace ongoing technological advancements to enhance operational efficiency, user experience, and overall infrastructure resilience.
   - Future-Proof Infrastructure: Integrate technologies with a focus on future standards, ensuring compatibility with evolving electric vehicle models and industry protocols.

3. Environmental Sustainability Practices:
   - Green Initiatives:
   - Renewable Energy Integration: Explore opportunities to integrate renewable energy sources into charging infrastructure, aligning with sustainability goals and potentially reducing long-term operational costs.
   - Carbon Footprint Reduction: Implement measures to reduce the carbon footprint of the charging network, contributing to environmental sustainability and enhancing the business's public image.

4. Community Engagement and Local Relationships:
   - Building Trust and Loyalty:

- Community Partnerships: Foster strong relationships with local communities through engagement initiatives, creating a sense of ownership and support for the charging infrastructure.

- Customer Loyalty Programs: Implement loyalty programs to encourage repeat usage, enhancing long-term user engagement and financial sustainability.

5. Diversification of Revenue Streams:
  - Income Source Variation:
  - New Revenue Models: Explore and diversify revenue streams by introducing innovative pricing models, subscription plans, or partnerships, ensuring financial stability in the face of changing market dynamics.

  - Adaptability to Industry Changes: Establish adaptable revenue models that can evolve with the industry, allowing the business to navigate shifts in user behavior and industry trends.

6. Regulatory Compliance and Incentives Utilization:
  - Strategic Use of Incentives:
  - Maximizing Government Support: Leverage government incentives, grants, and environmental certifications strategically to enhance financial viability while aligning with regulatory standards.

  - Compliance Monitoring: Stay vigilant about evolving regulatory requirements, ensuring continuous compliance and maximizing opportunities for financial incentives.

7. Employee Training and Skill Development:
  - Workforce Preparedness:
  - Adaptive Workforce: Invest in ongoing employee training to ensure the workforce remains adaptable to

technological changes and capable of delivering high-quality service.

    - Skill Enhancement Programs: Implement skill enhancement programs to empower employees with the capabilities needed for evolving roles within the organization.

8. Continuous Market Analysis:
    - Proactive Decision-Making:
    - Competitor Monitoring: Continuously analyze the competitive landscape, staying informed about new entrants, emerging technologies, and shifts in user expectations to make proactive business decisions.

    - User Feedback Integration: Actively gather and integrate user feedback to adapt services and amenities based on evolving user needs and expectations.

9. Financial Resilience:
    - Contingency Planning:
    - Risk Mitigation Strategies: Develop robust contingency plans to address potential challenges, ensuring financial resilience during economic fluctuations, regulatory changes, or unexpected events.

    - Scenario Analysis: Conduct scenario analyses to anticipate potential financial scenarios, allowing the business to adapt and implement strategic measures proactively.

Conclusion:

Long-term sustainability in the EV charging business requires a holistic approach that combines strategic planning, technology innovation, environmental sustainability, community engagement, and adaptability to market dynamics. By fostering financial viability and resilience, businesses can position themselves as key players in the evolving electric vehicle charging industry while contributing to the broader goals of environmental sustainability and user satisfaction.

CHAPTER 05

BUILDING A CHARGING STATION

Building a Charging Station: Unleashing the Power of Electric Mobility

1. Design and Construction Considerations:

- Strategic Site Selection:

- Optimal Locations: Choose sites with high visibility, accessibility, and diverse user traffic to maximize the charging station's impact.

- Urban and Suburban Presence: Ensure a strategic mix of locations in both urban and suburban settings to cater to various user needs.

- Scalability and Future Expansion:

- Modular Infrastructure: Design stations with scalability, allowing for the seamless addition of charging units as demand grows.

- Technology Integration: Employ future-ready technology to accommodate evolving charging standards and user expectations.

- User Experience and Amenities:

- User-Centric Design: Prioritize a user-friendly layout, intuitive charging interfaces, and a well-designed station environment.

- Enhanced Amenities: Provide amenities like comfortable waiting areas, Wi-Fi, and charging station information to enhance the overall user experience.

- Environmental Considerations:

- Sustainable Practices: Incorporate sustainable design elements, such as solar panels and energy-efficient lighting, aligning the charging station with environmental goals.

- Green Initiatives: Integrate eco-friendly features to reduce the station's carbon footprint and contribute to environmental conservation.

2. Permitting and Regulatory Hurdles:

  - Understanding Local Regulations:

    - Zoning Compliance: Navigate zoning laws to secure compliance with land use regulations and obtain necessary permits.

    - Building Code Adherence: Ensure adherence to local building codes and regulations, obtaining the required permits for construction and operation.

  - Environmental Impact Assessments:

    - Comprehensive Assessments: Conduct thorough environmental impact assessments, addressing concerns and implementing mitigation measures.

    - Community Involvement: Engage with the local community during the permitting process, promoting transparency and addressing potential environmental or community impacts.

  - Coordination with Utilities:

    - Power Supply Coordination: Collaborate with local utilities to secure ample power supply and obtain approvals for grid connections.

    - Utility Permits: Obtain necessary permits from utilities for any infrastructure affecting or connecting to existing utility systems.

  - Public and Private Partnerships:

- Government Collaboration: Explore partnerships with governmental bodies to streamline permitting processes and gain support for charging infrastructure initiatives.

- Private Sector Engagement: Collaborate with private entities to share resources and expertise, navigating regulatory hurdles more effectively.

3. Safety and Accessibility:

   - Safety Protocols:

   - Electrical Safety Measures: Implement stringent electrical safety measures, including regular inspections and compliance with industry standards.

   - Emergency Response Planning: Develop comprehensive emergency response plans to address potential incidents and prioritize user safety.

   - Accessibility Standards:

   - ADA Compliance: Ensure compliance with the Americans with Disabilities Act (ADA) guidelines, making charging stations accessible to individuals with disabilities.

   - Inclusive Design: Prioritize inclusivity in station design, ensuring accessibility for users of all abilities.

   - Security Measures:

   - Surveillance Systems: Install effective surveillance systems to enhance security and deter vandalism or unauthorized access.

125

- User Safety Features: Incorporate safety features like well-lit areas, emergency buttons, and visible security signage.

- User Education and Awareness:

- Informative Signage: Display clear signage providing information on safety procedures, charging guidelines, and emergency contacts.

- Training Programs: Offer user training programs to promote safe and efficient use of the charging infrastructure.

Conclusion:

Building a charging station requires a holistic approach, from strategic design and construction to navigating regulatory challenges and prioritizing safety and accessibility. By focusing on these key considerations, charging station operators can create a reliable and user-friendly infrastructure that contributes to the growth of electric mobility.

Importance of Design and Construction Considerations for Charging Stations

1. Strategic Site Selection:

- Optimal Accessibility: Careful site selection ensures that charging stations are easily accessible to a broad user base, maximizing their utilization and impact.

- Visibility: Strategic placement in high-traffic areas enhances visibility, attracting more users and promoting the adoption of electric vehicles.

2. Scalability and Future Expansion:

- Adaptability to Demand: Designing with scalability in mind allows for seamless expansion, ensuring the charging station can meet growing demand for electric vehicles.

- Technological Evolution: Future-ready infrastructure accommodates emerging charging standards and technological advancements, preventing obsolescence.

3. User Experience and Amenities:

- Enhanced Adoption: A user-friendly design and amenities contribute to a positive charging experience, encouraging repeat usage and fostering trust in electric mobility.

- Comfort and Convenience: Providing amenities like seating areas and Wi-Fi enhances user comfort and convenience, making the charging process more enjoyable.

4. Environmental Considerations:

- Sustainability Impact: Incorporating sustainable practices aligns the charging station with environmental goals, contributing to a green and eco-friendly image.

- Energy Efficiency: Utilizing energy-efficient lighting and renewable energy sources minimizes the station's environmental footprint.

In summary, meticulous design and construction considerations are crucial for charging stations to:

- Maximize Accessibility and Adoption: Strategic site selection ensures that charging stations are conveniently located, attracting a diverse user base and promoting the widespread adoption of electric vehicles.

- Future-Proof Infrastructure: Scalability and the integration of future-ready technology prevent infrastructure obsolescence, allowing charging stations to adapt to evolving industry standards and technological advancements.

- Enhance User Experience: A user-centric design and thoughtful amenities contribute to a positive charging experience, encouraging users to embrace electric mobility and fostering long-term user loyalty.

- Align with Sustainability Goals: Environmental considerations, such as sustainable design practices and energy-efficient features, position charging stations as eco-friendly and contribute to broader environmental conservation efforts.

By prioritizing these considerations, charging station operators can build infrastructure that not only meets current needs but also anticipates and accommodates the future growth of electric mobility.

Necessity of Strategic Site Selection for Charging Stations

1. Maximizing User Visibility:

- High-Traffic Areas: Choosing locations with high footfall or frequent vehicle traffic ensures that the charging station gains maximum visibility among potential users.

- Optimal Exposure: High-traffic areas provide an ideal platform for promoting electric vehicle adoption, reaching a diverse audience and raising awareness about the benefits of electric mobility.

2. Accessibility for Diverse Users:

- Urban and Suburban Presence: Considering diverse settings, including urban centers and suburban areas, ensures accessibility for a wide range of users.

- Meeting Varied Needs: Urban locations cater to users in densely populated areas, while suburban presence accommodates those in residential and commercial districts, meeting the varied charging needs of different demographics.

3. Encouraging User Adoption:

- Convenience and Accessibility: Strategic site selection prioritizes user convenience by placing charging stations in locations easily accessible during daily routines.

- Increased Usage Rates: By being present in high-traffic areas, charging stations become more convenient for users, encouraging frequent use and fostering the adoption of electric vehicles.

4. Supporting Urban and Suburban Lifestyles:

- Urban Efficiency: Urban locations cater to users with shorter commutes and higher population density, aligning with the efficiency and convenience associated with urban living.

- Suburban Accessibility: Suburban presence accommodates users in areas with larger residential spaces and longer commuting distances, providing accessibility for those with diverse lifestyle preferences.

5. Community Integration:

- Local Engagement: Placing charging stations in strategic locations fosters integration within local communities, promoting a sense of ownership and support for electric mobility initiatives.

- Community Awareness: High-visibility locations contribute to community awareness, encouraging residents to embrace sustainable transportation options and actively participate in the transition to electric vehicles.

In summary, strategic site selection is necessary for charging stations to:

- Maximize Visibility and Exposure: Placing charging stations in high-traffic areas ensures optimal visibility, reaching a broad audience and increasing awareness about electric vehicle charging options.

- Enhance Accessibility: Choosing locations in both urban and suburban settings accommodates diverse user needs, ensuring that charging stations are easily accessible to individuals with varied lifestyles and commuting patterns.

- Encourage Regular Usage: Conveniently located charging stations in high-traffic areas encourage regular usage, fostering the adoption of electric vehicles by providing accessible and visible charging options for users.

Scalability and Future Expansion in Charging Stations: Building for Growth

1. Modular Infrastructure:

- Adapting to Demand: Designing charging stations with scalability in mind enables the seamless addition of more charging units, ensuring the infrastructure can adapt to the growing demand for electric vehicle charging.

- Flexible Growth: Modular infrastructure allows operators to incrementally expand the station's capacity based on usage patterns and the increasing number of electric vehicles on the road.

2. Future-Ready Technology:

- Technological Evolution: Integrating infrastructure that accommodates evolving technology is crucial for staying abreast of advancements in electric vehicle charging standards.

- Charging Standard Compatibility: Future-ready technology ensures compatibility with emerging charging standards, preventing the need for significant infrastructure overhauls as technology evolves.

Importance:

1. Adaptability to Demand:

- Meeting Growing Demand: Scalable infrastructure caters to the increasing demand for electric vehicle charging services, preventing capacity constraints and accommodating a rising number of users.

- Flexibility in Expansion: Future growth can be efficiently managed by adding modular components, optimizing resource utilization and minimizing the need for extensive construction.

2. Technological Advancements:

- Staying Current: Future-ready technology positions charging stations to incorporate technological advancements seamlessly, offering users the latest features and ensuring compatibility with new electric vehicle models.

- Long-Term Viability: By investing in infrastructure that supports technological evolution, charging stations remain relevant and competitive in a dynamic market.

3. Cost-Effective Expansion:

- Incremental Investment: Scalability allows for incremental investment in infrastructure, aligning with the actual growth in demand and optimizing financial resources.

- Reduced Retrofitting Costs: Future-ready technology minimizes the need for costly retrofitting or complete overhauls, streamlining the expansion process and reducing associated expenses.

4. User Satisfaction:

- Consistent Service Availability: Scalable and future-ready charging stations ensure consistent service availability, preventing congestion and long waiting times for users.

- Enhanced User Experience: By offering the latest charging technologies, users experience enhanced reliability, faster charging times, and improved overall satisfaction.

5. Industry Competitiveness:

- Leading the Market: Scalability and future-ready technology position charging stations as leaders in the industry, attracting users and potential partnerships seeking reliable, innovative, and adaptable charging solutions.

- Market Resilience: Stations that can evolve with the industry remain resilient, adapting to changing market dynamics and maintaining a competitive edge over time.

In conclusion, scalability and future-ready technology are imperative for charging stations to:

- Meet Growing Demand: Scalable infrastructure adapts to increasing demand, ensuring consistent service availability and preventing congestion at charging stations.

- Stay Technologically Relevant: Future-ready technology supports compatibility with evolving charging standards and technological advancements, enhancing user experience and maintaining long-term viability.

-    Optimize Resource Utilization: Incremental scalability allows for cost-effective expansion, optimizing resource utilization based on actual demand growth and reducing the need for extensive retrofitting.

Importance of User Experience and Amenities in Charging Stations

1. User-Friendly Design:

- Accessible Charging Experience: A user-friendly layout ensures that the charging process is straightforward, making it easy for both experienced and new electric vehicle users.

- Clear Signage: Clear signage contributes to a positive user experience by providing essential information about charging procedures, rates, and station features.

- Well-Lit Surroundings: Well-lit surroundings enhance safety and security, creating a welcoming environment for users during day and night.

2. Amenities:

- Enhancing Comfort: Seating areas and amenities contribute to a comfortable and enjoyable charging experience, making users more likely to choose electric vehicles and return to the charging station.

- Connectivity with Wi-Fi: Providing Wi-Fi enhances user convenience, allowing them to stay connected and productive while their vehicles charge.

- Charging Station Waiting Spaces: Dedicated waiting spaces accommodate users during peak times, reducing potential congestion and ensuring a positive experience.

Importance:

1. Positive First Impression:

- Encouraging Adoption: A user-friendly design and welcoming atmosphere create a positive first impression, encouraging individuals to adopt electric vehicles and use charging stations.

- Reducing Barriers: A seamless and comfortable charging experience minimizes potential barriers to electric vehicle adoption, contributing to increased usage rates.

2. Customer Loyalty:

- Repeat Usage: A positive user experience, combined with amenities, fosters customer loyalty, encouraging users to return to the same charging station for future charging needs.

- User Satisfaction: Satisfied users are more likely to recommend the charging station to others, contributing to word-of-mouth promotion and community support.

3. Attracting Diverse User Demographics:

- Meeting Varied Needs: Amenities cater to diverse user needs, attracting a wide range of demographics, from business professionals seeking Wi-Fi connectivity to families in need of comfortable waiting areas.

- Inclusive Design: Creating spaces that accommodate various preferences and requirements contributes to an inclusive charging environment.

4. Competitive Edge:

- Differentiation in the Market: Charging stations that prioritize user experience and amenities differentiate themselves in the market, gaining a competitive edge and attracting users seeking a superior charging experience.

- Community Support: Positive user experiences contribute to community support, generating goodwill and fostering a positive relationship between the charging station and the local community.

5. Promoting Electric Mobility Lifestyle:

- Creating a Lifestyle Experience: Amenities enhance the charging station visit into a positive lifestyle experience, contributing to the perception of electric mobility as convenient, modern, and enjoyable.

- Cultural Shift: By making electric vehicle charging enjoyable, stations contribute to the cultural shift towards sustainable and eco-friendly transportation.

In summary, user experience and amenities are crucial for charging stations to:

- Encourage Adoption: A positive user experience reduces barriers to electric vehicle adoption, encouraging individuals to choose electric mobility and use charging stations.

- Build Customer Loyalty: Amenities and a welcoming atmosphere foster customer loyalty, encouraging repeat usage and positive recommendations to others.

- Attract Diverse Demographics: Amenities cater to diverse user needs, attracting a wide range of users with varied preferences and requirements.

- Gain a Competitive Edge: Prioritizing user experience differentiates charging stations in the market, contributing to a competitive advantage and community support.

Necessity of Environmental Considerations in Charging Stations

1. Sustainable Design:

- Reducing Environmental Impact: Incorporating sustainable and eco-friendly design elements, such as solar panels or green roofs, aligns charging stations with broader environmental goals.

- Promoting Renewable Energy: Utilizing sustainable design features promotes the use of renewable energy sources, contributing to a reduction in carbon emissions associated with electric vehicle charging.

2. Energy-Efficient Lighting:

- Minimizing Environmental Footprint: The use of energy-efficient lighting solutions not only enhances functionality but also minimizes the overall environmental footprint of the charging station.

- Resource Conservation: Energy-efficient lighting contributes to resource conservation by reducing energy consumption, aligning with principles of environmental sustainability.

Importance:

1. Aligning with Environmental Goals:

- Demonstrating Commitment: Sustainable design elements demonstrate a commitment to environmental responsibility, fostering positive perceptions among users, local communities, and regulatory bodies.

- Meeting Regulatory Standards: Many regions encourage or mandate sustainable practices, and charging stations that adhere to environmental guidelines are more likely to receive regulatory support and approval.

2. Reducing Carbon Footprint:

- Renewable Energy Integration: Incorporating renewable energy sources, such as solar panels, directly reduces the carbon footprint associated with charging electric vehicles.

- Contribution to Clean Energy Transition: Charging stations with sustainable features contribute to the broader transition to cleaner energy sources, supporting global efforts to combat climate change.

3. Promoting Green Technologies:

- Setting Industry Standards: Charging stations with sustainable features set a standard for environmentally conscious practices within the electric vehicle charging industry.

- Influencing User Behavior: Environmental considerations can influence user behavior, encouraging individuals to choose charging stations that prioritize sustainability and contribute to a greener future.

4. Cost Savings and Efficiency:

- Long-Term Cost Savings: Sustainable features, such as solar panels, can lead to long-term cost savings by harnessing renewable energy and reducing dependence on traditional power sources.

- Operational Efficiency: Energy-efficient lighting not only reduces environmental impact but also contributes to the operational efficiency of the charging station.

5. Enhancing Community Support:

- Community Engagement: Charging stations with sustainable design elements often receive positive community support, as they align with local and global efforts to promote environmentally friendly practices.

- Cultivating Goodwill: Positive environmental practices cultivate goodwill within the community, contributing to a positive perception of the charging station as a responsible and community-oriented facility.

In summary, environmental considerations are necessary for charging stations to:

- Demonstrate Environmental Responsibility: Sustainable design elements showcase a commitment to environmental responsibility, positively influencing perceptions among users, communities, and regulatory bodies.

- Reduce Carbon Footprint: Integrating renewable energy sources and energy-efficient technologies directly reduces the carbon footprint associated with charging electric vehicles, contributing to global efforts to combat climate change.

- Promote Industry Standards: Charging stations with sustainable features set industry standards for environmentally conscious practices, influencing user behavior and contributing to a green and sustainable future.

- Enhance Cost Savings and Efficiency: Sustainable features, such as solar panels and energy-efficient lighting, can lead to long-term cost savings and operational efficiency for charging stations.

- Cultivate Community Support: Positive environmental practices contribute to community support, fostering goodwill and positive perceptions of the charging station as a responsible and community-oriented facility.

Permitting and Regulatory Hurdles in Charging Station Development

1. Understanding Local Regulations:

- Navigating Complexities: Local regulations related to charging station development can be complex and vary across jurisdictions. Understanding these regulations is crucial for a smooth permitting process.

- Compliance Assurance: Understanding and adhering to local regulations ensure compliance, mitigating risks associated with penalties, delays, or legal challenges during and after construction.

2. Zoning and Land Use Regulations:

- Compliance with Land Use Requirements: Zoning laws dictate how land can be used and developed. Navigating these regulations is essential to ensure that the charging station complies with land use requirements and restrictions.

- Site Suitability: Understanding zoning laws helps in selecting suitable sites that align with the designated land use for charging station development.

3. Building Codes:

- Securing Necessary Permits: Adhering to local building codes and regulations is imperative to secure the necessary permits for construction and operation.

- Ensuring Structural Integrity: Compliance with building codes guarantees that the charging station meets structural and safety standards, ensuring the safety of users and the surrounding community.

Importance:

1. Compliance and Legal Certainty:

- Avoiding Legal Issues: Understanding local regulations helps in avoiding legal issues that may arise due to non-compliance, ensuring a legally secure and certifiable charging station development process.

- Risk Mitigation: Knowledge of local regulations allows developers to identify and mitigate potential risks early in the planning stages, preventing legal challenges during or after construction.

2. Community Acceptance:

- Building Community Trust: Adhering to zoning laws and building codes demonstrates a commitment to respecting the community's established norms and regulations, fostering trust and acceptance.

- Addressing Community Concerns: Compliance with local regulations helps address community concerns related to safety, aesthetics, and the overall impact of the charging station on the neighborhood.

3. Efficient Permitting Process:

- Streamlining Development: Understanding local regulations streamlines the permitting process, reducing delays and expediting the development timeline.

- Early Issue Identification: Awareness of regulations allows developers to identify potential issues early, addressing them proactively and preventing delays during the permitting phase.

4. Safety and Structural Integrity:

- Ensuring User Safety: Adherence to building codes ensures the structural integrity of the charging station, prioritizing user safety during operation.

- Mitigating Risks: Compliance with safety regulations minimizes the risk of accidents or incidents related to the charging station's construction and operation.

5. Government and Stakeholder Relations:

- Facilitating Government Support: Compliance with local regulations enhances the likelihood of receiving government support for charging station initiatives, leading to potential incentives or partnerships.

- Positive Stakeholder Engagement: Transparent adherence to regulations fosters positive stakeholder engagement, promoting cooperation and collaboration with local authorities and communities.

In summary, understanding local regulations, including zoning and land use regulations, and adhering to building codes is necessary for charging station development to:

- Ensure Compliance: Compliance with local regulations ensures legal certainty and mitigates the risk of legal challenges during or after construction.

- Build Community Trust: Adherence to regulations demonstrates respect for community norms, fostering trust and acceptance among local residents.

- Streamline Permitting: Knowledge of regulations streamlines the permitting process, reducing delays and expediting the development timeline.

- Prioritize Safety: Adherence to building codes ensures the safety and structural integrity of the charging station, prioritizing user safety during operation.

- Facilitate Government and Stakeholder Support: Compliance enhances the likelihood of receiving government support and promotes positive stakeholder engagement, facilitating successful charging station initiatives.

Environmental Impact Assessments in Charging Station Development

1. Environmental Compliance:

- Thorough Assessments: Environmental Impact Assessments (EIAs) involve a comprehensive evaluation of potential environmental impacts associated with charging station development.

- Mitigation Measures: The assessments identify potential environmental risks and propose mitigation measures to address and minimize any adverse effects on the environment.

2. Community Engagement:

- Transparent Permitting Process: Involving the local community in the permitting process enhances transparency, ensuring that residents are informed about the potential environmental impacts and mitigation efforts.

- Addressing Concerns: Community engagement provides a platform for addressing community concerns related to the environmental impact of the charging station, fostering a collaborative approach to sustainable development.

Importance:

1. Environmental Stewardship:

- Mitigating Impact: EIAs enable charging station developers to identify and mitigate potential environmental impacts, ensuring responsible and sustainable development.

- Reducing Ecological Footprint: Thorough environmental assessments contribute to minimizing the ecological footprint of charging station operations, aligning with environmental stewardship principles.

2. Legal Compliance:

- Meeting Regulatory Standards: Conducting EIAs demonstrates commitment to meeting regulatory standards related to environmental impact assessments, ensuring legal compliance.

- Avoiding Penalties: Adherence to environmental regulations mitigates the risk of legal penalties or project delays associated with non-compliance.

3. Community Relations:

- Building Trust: Thorough environmental assessments and community engagement build trust with the local community, fostering positive relations and support for charging station development.

- Addressing Concerns: Community engagement allows developers to address community concerns about potential environmental impacts, demonstrating responsiveness and a commitment to responsible development.

4. Sustainable Development:

- Balancing Growth and Environment: EIAs contribute to the achievement of sustainable development goals by balancing the growth of charging infrastructure with environmental conservation efforts.

- Long-Term Viability: Sustainable development practices, guided by environmental assessments, enhance the long-term viability of charging station operations by minimizing negative environmental consequences.

5. Public Perception and Support:

- Positive Public Perception: Transparent communication about environmental impacts and mitigation measures contributes to positive public perception of the charging station project.

- Gaining Community Support: Engaging with the community through EIAs and addressing environmental concerns helps in gaining community support, an essential element for successful charging station projects.

6. Risk Management:

- Identifying Potential Risks: Environmental impact assessments identify potential risks and hazards, allowing developers to proactively manage and mitigate environmental challenges.

- Contingency Planning: A comprehensive understanding of environmental impacts supports the development of effective contingency plans, ensuring a swift and effective response to unforeseen environmental issues.

In summary, environmental impact assessments are crucial for charging station development to:

- Demonstrate Environmental Responsibility: Conducting thorough EIAs demonstrates a commitment to environmental responsibility, minimizing adverse effects on the environment.

- Ensure Legal Compliance: Environmental impact assessments contribute to meeting regulatory standards, ensuring legal compliance and avoiding potential penalties.

- Build Community Trust: Community engagement through EIAs builds trust with the local community, addressing concerns and fostering positive relations for sustainable development.

- Support Sustainable Development: EIAs contribute to sustainable development by balancing growth with environmental conservation efforts, enhancing the long-term viability of charging station operations.

- Manage Risks Effectively: Identifying potential environmental risks allows for proactive risk management and

A Guide to the EV Charging Business

the development of contingency plans, ensuring a swift response to unforeseen challenges.

Importance of Coordination with Utilities in Charging Station Development

1. Power Supply Approval:

- Ensuring Sufficient Power Supply: Coordinating with local utilities is essential to ensure that the charging station has access to a sufficient and reliable power supply from the electrical grid.

- Securing Approvals: Utilities often require approval for new connections or increased load demand, and coordination ensures that the necessary approvals are secured before construction.

2. Utility Permits:

- Infrastructure Impact Assessment: Utilities manage the electrical infrastructure, and obtaining permits is crucial when the charging station's construction or operation impacts existing utility systems.

- Preventing Disruptions: Coordination helps in preventing disruptions to existing utility services and ensures that the charging station's infrastructure aligns with utility requirements.

Importance:

1. Power Supply Reliability:

- Avoiding Grid Overloads: Coordination with utilities ensures that the charging station's power demand aligns with the capacity of the local electrical grid, preventing overloads and maintaining grid reliability.

- Securing Adequate Capacity: Utilities can assess the available capacity and upgrade infrastructure if needed, ensuring that the charging station receives the required power without straining the grid.

2. Regulatory Compliance:

- Adherence to Utility Regulations: Utilities operate within regulatory frameworks, and coordination ensures compliance with regulations related to power supply, connections, and load demands.

- Avoiding Regulatory Hurdles: Failure to coordinate with utilities may lead to regulatory hurdles or delays in obtaining necessary approvals, impacting the charging station's development timeline.

3. Preventing Infrastructure Conflicts:

- Minimizing Impact on Existing Systems: Utility permits help in assessing and minimizing the impact of the charging station's infrastructure on existing utility systems, preventing conflicts and disruptions.

- Coordinated Development: Coordination fosters a collaborative approach, allowing the charging station's development to align seamlessly with utility infrastructure and services.

4. Operational Efficiency:

- Reliable Power Supply: Coordinated power supply ensures the operational efficiency of the charging station, preventing downtime and ensuring a reliable service for users.

- Avoiding Service Interruptions: Utility permits help in avoiding service interruptions for other utility customers, maintaining uninterrupted services for the broader community.

5. Cost Efficiency:

- Optimizing Infrastructure Development: Coordination with utilities helps in optimizing infrastructure development, preventing unnecessary expenses related to overhauls or upgrades that could have been avoided with early collaboration.

- Avoiding Retrofitting Costs: Early coordination reduces the likelihood of retrofitting or modifying infrastructure post-construction, minimizing associated costs.

6. Community Impact:

- Mitigating Disruptions: Coordinated development mitigates disruptions to the local community by preventing unexpected interruptions to existing utility services.

- Enhancing Community Support: A well-coordinated approach, considering the impact on utilities, contributes to positive community support for the charging station project.

In summary, coordination with utilities is crucial for charging station development to:

- Ensure Power Supply Reliability: Coordinated planning ensures that the charging station receives a reliable and sufficient power supply without overloading the local electrical grid.

- Achieve Regulatory Compliance: Coordination with utilities ensures compliance with regulations related to power supply, connections, and load demands.

- Prevent Infrastructure Conflicts: Utility permits help in assessing and minimizing the impact of the charging station's infrastructure on existing utility systems, preventing conflicts and disruptions.

- Optimize Operational Efficiency: Coordinated power supply and infrastructure development contribute to the operational efficiency of the charging station, avoiding downtime and ensuring reliable service.

- Enhance Cost Efficiency: Early coordination with utilities helps in optimizing infrastructure development, avoiding unnecessary expenses and retrofitting costs.

- Mitigate Community Impact: Coordinated development minimizes disruptions to the local community by preventing unexpected interruptions to existing utility services, enhancing community support for the charging station project.

Public and Private Partnerships in Charging Station Development

1. Government Collaboration:

- Streamlining Permitting Process: Collaborating with government entities facilitates a smoother permitting process for charging station development, leveraging governmental support to navigate regulatory requirements.

- Access to Incentives: Partnerships with government entities may provide access to incentives, grants, or funding programs that support the development of charging infrastructure.

- Policy Advocacy: Government collaborations allow for active involvement in policy advocacy, influencing regulations and standards to promote the growth of the electric vehicle charging sector.

2. Private Sector Collaboration:

- Shared Resources: Collaborating with private entities enables the sharing of resources, including expertise, technology, and funding, which can enhance the efficiency and effectiveness of charging station projects.

- Expertise in Regulatory Affairs: Private sector collaboration brings in expertise in navigating regulatory hurdles, ensuring that charging station developers benefit from industry knowledge and experience.

- Accelerating Innovation: Private sector partnerships foster innovation by integrating advancements in technology and business models, contributing to the evolution of the charging infrastructure sector.

Importance:

1. Accelerating Project Development:

   - Government Support: Collaboration with government entities expedites project development by streamlining bureaucratic processes, reducing delays in permitting, and ensuring timely approvals.

   - Private Sector Efficiency: Private sector collaboration accelerates project timelines by leveraging the efficiency and agility of private entities in navigating regulatory challenges and deploying resources effectively.

2. Access to Funding and Incentives:

   - Government Funding: Partnerships with government entities provide access to funding programs and incentives, supporting the financial aspects of charging station projects.

   - Private Sector Investment: Private sector collaboration can attract investment from private entities, ensuring the availability of capital for infrastructure development, technology upgrades, and expansion.

3. Mitigating Regulatory Challenges:

   - Government Advocacy: Collaboration with government entities enables proactive advocacy for supportive policies, addressing regulatory challenges that may hinder the growth of charging infrastructure.

   - Private Sector Expertise: Private sector collaboration brings regulatory expertise, ensuring that developers navigate complex regulatory landscapes efficiently and compliantly.

4. Resource Optimization:

- Government Resources: Collaboration with government entities allows charging station developers to leverage government resources, including land, utilities, and existing infrastructure, optimizing resource utilization.

- Private Sector Innovation: Private sector collaboration brings innovative solutions and technology, optimizing the deployment of charging infrastructure and enhancing user experience.

5. Holistic Ecosystem Development:

- Integrated Approach: Public and private partnerships facilitate a holistic approach to ecosystem development, integrating government initiatives with private sector innovation for a comprehensive charging infrastructure network.

- Balancing Interests: Collaboration ensures a balanced consideration of public and private interests, creating an ecosystem that meets regulatory requirements while fostering business growth.

6. Long-Term Sustainability:

- Government Policies: Collaboration with government entities aligns projects with long-term policy objectives, ensuring sustained support and regulatory stability for charging infrastructure.

- Private Sector Viability: Private sector collaboration enhances the long-term viability of charging infrastructure projects by bringing financial sustainability and innovation to the sector.

In summary, public and private partnerships are essential for charging station development to:

- Accelerate Project Development: Collaboration with government and private entities expedites project timelines by streamlining regulatory processes and providing access to resources.

- Access Funding and Incentives: Partnerships with government entities and private sector collaboration ensure access to funding programs, incentives, and private investment to support charging infrastructure projects.

- Mitigate Regulatory Challenges: Government collaboration enables policy advocacy, while private sector expertise helps navigate complex regulatory landscapes efficiently.

- Optimize Resource Utilization: Collaboration allows for the optimization of resources, leveraging government resources and private sector innovation for efficient charging infrastructure deployment.

- Develop a Holistic Ecosystem: Public and private partnerships create a holistic ecosystem, integrating government initiatives with private sector innovation for a comprehensive charging infrastructure network.

- Ensure Long-Term Sustainability: Collaboration with both government and private entities aligns projects with long-term policy objectives, ensuring sustained support and regulatory stability for charging infrastructure.

Safety and Accessibility in Charging Station Development

1. Safety:

- User Safety: Ensuring that the charging station design and construction prioritize user safety, preventing accidents or hazards during charging.

- Compliance with Standards: Adhering to safety standards and regulations to create a secure environment for users and minimize risks associated with electrical systems.

- Emergency Protocols: Implementing clear emergency protocols, including response plans and safety signage, to address unexpected situations promptly.

- Regular Inspections: Conduct regular inspections and maintenance to identify and address potential safety concerns, ensuring ongoing safety compliance.

2. Accessibility:

- Universal Design: Designing charging stations with universal accessibility in mind, accommodating users with diverse needs, including those with physical disabilities.

- Location Accessibility: Choosing locations that are easily accessible to a wide range of users, considering factors such as proximity to main roads, public transportation, and urban centers.

- User-Friendly Interfaces: Developing user-friendly interfaces for charging equipment, ensuring ease of use for individuals with varying levels of technological expertise.

- Consideration of Special Needs: Taking into account special needs, such as additional amenities or services, to make the charging experience inclusive for all users.

Importance:

1. User Safety:

- Preventing Accidents: Prioritizing safety in charging station development prevents accidents, electrical hazards, or other incidents that could pose risks to users.

- Building Trust: Emphasizing safety measures builds trust among users, fostering a positive perception of the charging station and encouraging repeat usage.

2. Compliance with Regulations:

- Legal Compliance: Adhering to safety regulations ensures legal compliance, mitigating the risk of penalties or legal challenges related to safety standards.

- Risk Management: Implementing safety measures is a critical aspect of risk management, reducing the likelihood of accidents and associated liabilities.

3. Emergency Preparedness:

- Quick Response: Having clear emergency protocols ensures a quick and effective response to unforeseen situations, minimizing the impact of emergencies on user safety.

- User Confidence: Users are more likely to have confidence in the charging station's reliability if they know that safety measures and emergency procedures are in place.

4. Accessibility for All Users:

- Inclusive Charging Experience: Designing charging stations with universal accessibility creates an inclusive charging experience, accommodating users with varying needs.

- Enhanced User Experience: Accessibility features contribute to an enhanced overall user experience, making the charging station welcoming and usable for a diverse user base.

5. Location Considerations:

- Convenient Access: Choosing accessible locations enhances the convenience for users, encouraging usage and contributing to the success of the charging station.

- Promoting Electric Vehicle Adoption: Accessible locations make electric vehicle charging more attractive and feasible for a broader audience, promoting the adoption of electric vehicles.

6. User-Friendly Interfaces:

- Ease of Use: User-friendly interfaces ensure that individuals with varying technological expertise can easily operate the charging equipment, promoting widespread adoption.

- Positive User Experience: A positive user experience encourages users to return to the charging station, contributing to the station's success and reputation.

7. Universal Design:

- Inclusivity: Universal design principles ensure that charging stations are accessible to everyone, regardless of physical abilities, contributing to social inclusivity.

- Meeting Diverse Needs: Considering diverse user needs promotes a more welcoming and supportive environment for all individuals using the charging station.

8. Regular Inspections and Maintenance:

- Preventive Measures: Regular inspections and maintenance help identify and address potential safety concerns before they escalate, ensuring ongoing safety and functionality.

- Long-Term Reliability: Consistent safety measures and maintenance contribute to the long-term reliability of the charging station, reducing downtime and ensuring uninterrupted service.

In summary, safety and accessibility in charging station development are crucial to:

- Prioritize User Safety: Implementing measures to prevent accidents and hazards, building trust among users and ensuring legal compliance.

- Ensure Legal Compliance: Adhering to safety regulations to mitigate the risk of penalties or legal challenges related to safety standards.

- Facilitate Emergency Preparedness: Having clear emergency protocols to ensure a quick and effective response to unforeseen situations, promoting user confidence.

- Create an Inclusive Charging Experience: Designing charging stations with universal accessibility to accommodate users with diverse needs, enhancing the overall user experience.

- Choose Accessible Locations: Selecting locations that are easily accessible to a wide range of users, contributing to the convenience and success of the charging station.

- Promote User-Friendly Interfaces: Developing user-friendly interfaces to ensure ease of use for individuals with varying levels of technological expertise.

- Adopt Universal Design Principles: Designing charging stations with universal design principles to create an inclusive and welcoming environment for all users.

- Conduct Regular Inspections and Maintenance: Regularly inspecting and maintaining charging stations to identify and address potential safety concerns, ensuring ongoing safety and reliability.

Safety Protocols in Charging Station Development

1. Electrical Safety:

- Rigorous Inspections: Implement regular and thorough electrical inspections to identify potential hazards, ensuring the charging station's electrical systems comply with safety standards.

- Compliance with Standards: Adhere to industry safety standards for electrical systems, ensuring that the charging infrastructure is designed, installed, and maintained in compliance with recognized safety regulations.

- Equipment Certification: Use certified and tested charging equipment to prevent electrical faults and ensure the safety of users and the charging station.

2. Emergency Response Plans:

- Comprehensive Plans: Develop and maintain comprehensive emergency response plans that outline procedures for various potential incidents, such as electrical malfunctions, accidents, or natural disasters.

- User Education: Educate users about emergency response protocols, providing clear instructions on what to do in case of an emergency to enhance overall user safety.

- Collaboration with Authorities: Coordinate with local authorities and emergency services to ensure seamless collaboration and effective response in the event of an emergency.

Importance:

1. Electrical Safety:

- Preventing Electrical Hazards: Rigorous electrical safety measures prevent electrical hazards, reducing the risk of accidents, injuries, or damage to the charging infrastructure.

- User Confidence: Adhering to safety standards instills confidence in users, assuring them that the charging station is designed and maintained with their safety in mind.

2. Emergency Response Plans:

- Swift Response to Incidents: Comprehensive emergency response plans enable a swift and organized response to various incidents, minimizing potential harm and ensuring user safety.

- User Awareness: Educating users about emergency response protocols enhances user awareness, empowering them to take appropriate actions during unexpected situations.

Implementation:

1. Electrical Safety:

- Regular Inspections: Conduct regular electrical inspections, including checks on charging equipment, wiring, and connections, to identify and rectify potential safety hazards promptly.

- Training for Maintenance Personnel: Provide training to maintenance personnel on electrical safety procedures, ensuring that they are equipped to handle and address potential issues.

- Certification Requirements: Ensure that all electrical components, including charging equipment, meet relevant safety certifications and standards, preventing substandard equipment from being part of the charging station.

2. Emergency Response Plans:

- Scenario-Based Planning: Develop emergency response plans based on various scenarios, including electrical malfunctions, fires, medical emergencies, or natural disasters.

- User Communication Channels: Establish clear communication channels with users, such as signage and digital notifications, to convey emergency procedures and contact information for assistance.

- Regular Drills and Training: Conduct regular emergency response drills and training sessions for staff and relevant stakeholders to ensure a well-coordinated and efficient response in real-life situations.

Benefits:

1. Electrical Safety:

- User Protection: Rigorous electrical safety measures prioritize user protection, minimizing the risk of electrical accidents or malfunctions during the charging process.

- Infrastructure Reliability: Compliance with industry standards ensures the reliability of the charging station's electrical infrastructure, reducing the likelihood of disruptions or faults.

2. Emergency Response Plans:

- Minimizing Impact: Comprehensive emergency response plans minimize the impact of incidents on users and the charging station, safeguarding both physical safety and operational continuity.

- Building User Trust: Transparent communication and user education about emergency response plans build trust, fostering a positive perception of the charging station and its commitment to user safety.

In summary, safety protocols in charging station development, including electrical safety measures and emergency response plans, are crucial to:

- Prioritize User Safety: Rigorous electrical inspections and compliance with safety standards prioritize user safety and instill confidence in the charging station's reliability.

- Minimize Impact of Incidents: Comprehensive emergency response plans minimize the impact of incidents, safeguarding both user safety and the operational continuity of the charging station.

- Educate and Build Trust: User education about safety protocols and transparent communication builds trust, contributing to a positive user perception and confidence in the charging station's commitment to safety.

Accessibility Standards in Charging Station Development

1. ADA Compliance:

- Americans with Disabilities Act (ADA): Design charging stations in compliance with the Americans with Disabilities Act (ADA) to ensure accessibility for individuals with disabilities.

- Accessibility Guidelines: Adhere to ADA guidelines, which include specifications for parking spaces, pathways, and charging equipment to accommodate users with diverse abilities.

2. Inclusive Design:

- Prioritizing Inclusivity: Prioritize inclusivity in the design of charging stations, ensuring that features and infrastructure are accessible and usable for individuals of all abilities.

- Universal Design Principles: Apply universal design principles to create an environment that accommodates a diverse range of users, regardless of physical capabilities.

Importance:

1. ADA Compliance:

- Legal Requirement: ADA compliance is a legal requirement to ensure equal access for individuals with disabilities, preventing discrimination and promoting accessibility in public spaces.

- Enhancing User Experience: ADA-compliant design enhances the overall user experience, making charging stations welcoming and accessible to a broader user base.

2. Inclusive Design:

- User-Friendly Environment: Inclusive design ensures that charging stations create a user-friendly environment for everyone, promoting a positive and accessible experience for users with different abilities.

- Encouraging EV Adoption: An accessible charging infrastructure encourages a wider audience, including individuals with disabilities, to consider electric vehicle adoption.

Implementation:

1. ADA Compliance:

- Accessible Parking Spaces: Design and allocate accessible parking spaces according to ADA specifications, ensuring proper dimensions and proximity to charging equipment.

- Pathway Accessibility: Ensure that pathways leading to and around charging stations are accessible, with smooth surfaces, appropriate slopes, and clear signage.

- Accessible Charging Equipment: Install charging equipment at heights and locations accessible to individuals with disabilities, considering reach ranges and clear floor spaces.

2. Inclusive Design:

- Universal Design Features: Incorporate universal design features, such as easy-to-use interfaces, clear signage, and well-lit areas, to create a welcoming environment for users of all abilities.

- Consideration of Diverse Needs: Consider diverse user needs, including those related to mobility, vision, and hearing, when designing charging station amenities and facilities.

- User Input: Seek input from individuals with disabilities or advocacy groups during the design phase to address specific accessibility considerations and improve the overall inclusivity of the charging station.

Benefits:

1. ADA Compliance:

- Legal Compliance: ADA compliance ensures that charging stations adhere to legal requirements, reducing the risk of legal challenges related to accessibility.

- Positive Public Perception: Complying with ADA standards contributes to a positive public perception, showcasing the charging station's commitment to inclusivity and accessibility.

2. Inclusive Design:

- Enhanced User Experience: Inclusive design enhances the overall user experience, making charging stations more user-friendly and accommodating for a diverse range of users.

- Expanded User Base: An accessible and inclusive charging infrastructure attracts a broader user base, promoting electric vehicle adoption among individuals with diverse abilities.

In summary, adherence to accessibility standards, including ADA compliance and inclusive design principles, is crucial to:

- Ensure Legal Compliance: ADA compliance ensures that charging stations meet legal requirements related to accessibility, reducing the risk of legal challenges.

- Enhance User Experience: Inclusive design enhances the overall user experience, making charging stations more user-friendly and accommodating for individuals with diverse abilities.

- Promote Positive Public Perception: ADA compliance and inclusive design contribute to a positive public perception, showcasing the charging station's commitment to inclusivity and accessibility.

- Expand User Base: An accessible and inclusive charging infrastructure attracts a broader user base, encouraging electric vehicle adoption among individuals with diverse abilities.

Security Measures in Charging Station Development

1. Surveillance Systems:

- CCTV Installation: Install Closed-Circuit Television (CCTV) cameras strategically to monitor and record activities around the charging station, enhancing security.

- Deterrent Effect: The presence of visible surveillance systems acts as a deterrent, discouraging potential vandals or unauthorized individuals from engaging in malicious activities.

2. User Safety Features:

- Well-Lit Areas: Ensure well-lit surroundings at the charging station to enhance visibility and create a safer environment for users during day and night.

- Emergency Buttons: Install emergency buttons or communication devices that users can easily access in case of any safety concerns, facilitating prompt assistance.

- Visible Security Signage: Display visible security signage to communicate the presence of security measures, promoting a sense of safety among users.

Importance:

1. Surveillance Systems:

- Preventing Vandalism: Surveillance systems act as a deterrent, reducing the likelihood of vandalism, theft, or unauthorized access to charging station equipment.

- Evidence Collection: CCTV cameras provide a means to collect evidence in the event of incidents, aiding law enforcement and ensuring accountability for any security breaches.

2. User Safety Features:

- Enhancing User Safety: Well-lit areas, emergency buttons, and visible security signage contribute to user safety, creating a secure environment that encourages user confidence.

- Emergency Response Facilitation: Emergency buttons facilitate quick communication and response, allowing users to summon assistance in case of safety or security concerns.

Implementation:

1. Surveillance Systems:

- Strategic Camera Placement: Install CCTV cameras at key locations, including charging equipment areas, entry points, and parking spaces, to provide comprehensive coverage.

- Remote Monitoring: Implement remote monitoring capabilities for surveillance systems, allowing real-time observation of charging station activities and immediate response to security incidents.

2. User Safety Features:

- Adequate Lighting: Ensure proper lighting throughout the charging station premises, utilizing energy-efficient and reliable lighting solutions to maintain visibility.

- Accessible Emergency Buttons: Install emergency buttons in easily accessible locations, ensuring that users can quickly reach them in case of emergencies.

- Clear Signage: Display clear and visible security signage, indicating the presence of surveillance systems, emergency buttons, and other safety features to inform users and deter potential threats.

Benefits:

1. Surveillance Systems:

- Reducing Security Risks: Surveillance systems reduce security risks by deterring potential threats and providing a means for prompt response to unauthorized activities.

- Enhanced Accountability: In the event of security incidents, CCTV footage serves as valuable evidence, aiding law enforcement and promoting accountability.

2. User Safety Features:

- User Confidence: Well-lit areas, emergency buttons, and visible security signage enhance user confidence in the safety of the charging station, encouraging repeat usage.

- Effective Emergency Response: User safety features contribute to an effective emergency response, allowing users to quickly and easily seek assistance when needed.

In summary, security measures, including surveillance systems and user safety features, are crucial to:

- Prevent Security Threats: Surveillance systems act as a deterrent, reducing the likelihood of vandalism, theft, or unauthorized access to charging station equipment.

- Enhance User Safety: Well-lit areas, emergency buttons, and visible security signage contribute to user safety, creating a secure environment that encourages user confidence.

- Provide Evidence in Incidents: CCTV cameras provide evidence in the event of security incidents, aiding law enforcement and ensuring accountability for security breaches.

- Facilitate Emergency Response: User safety features, such as emergency buttons, facilitate quick communication and response, allowing users to summon assistance in case of safety or security concerns.

Importance of User Education and Awareness in Charging Station Development

1. Educational Signage:

- Safety Procedures: Clear signage communicates safety procedures, ensuring users are informed about proper conduct and emergency protocols while using the charging station.

- Charging Protocols: Informative signage guides users on the correct charging protocols, minimizing the risk of errors or misuse that could affect safety or equipment functionality.

- Emergency Contacts: Displaying emergency contacts provides users with quick access to assistance if needed, contributing to a safer charging environment.

2. User Training Programs:

- Safe Usage: Training programs educate users on safe and efficient usage of the charging infrastructure, reducing the likelihood of accidents or damage caused by user error.

- Efficient Charging Practices: Promoting efficient charging practices helps users optimize their charging experience, minimizing waiting times and maximizing station utilization.

- Awareness of Features: Users trained through programs are more aware of available features, such as emergency buttons or user support, contributing to a smoother and safer charging process.

Benefits:

1. Educational Signage:

- Enhanced User Safety: Educational signage enhances user safety by providing clear guidance on safety procedures, emergency contacts, and proper charging protocols.

- Reduced Misuse: Clear instructions reduce the risk of user error or misuse, preventing incidents that could impact the safety and functionality of the charging station.

2. User Training Programs:

- Safe and Efficient Charging: User training programs ensure that users understand how to use the charging infrastructure safely and efficiently, contributing to a positive charging experience.

- Optimized Station Utilization: Educated users are more likely to follow efficient charging practices, contributing to optimized station utilization and reduced waiting times for other users.

- User Empowerment: Training programs empower users with knowledge about available features and support, enabling them to navigate the charging process confidently.

Implementation:

1. Educational Signage:

- Strategic Placement: Place educational signage at key locations, including charging stations, entry points, and waiting areas, ensuring maximum visibility for users.

- Multilingual Information: Consider providing information in multiple languages to cater to a diverse user base and enhance accessibility.

2. User Training Programs:

- Online Resources: Develop online resources, such as video tutorials or user manuals, that users can access to familiarize themselves with charging protocols and safety procedures.

- On-Site Workshops: Conduct on-site workshops or information sessions periodically to offer hands-on training and address user questions or concerns directly.

User Awareness:

1. Educational Signage:

- Promoting Safety Culture: Educational signage contributes to a safety-conscious culture among users, fostering a sense of responsibility for their own safety and the safety of others.

- User Confidence: Clear instructions and emergency contacts on signage enhance user confidence in using the charging station, creating a positive user experience.

2. User Training Programs:

- Empowering Users: User training programs empower users with knowledge, making them more self-sufficient and capable of navigating the charging process independently.

- Promoting Responsible Usage: Training programs promote responsible usage, encouraging users to adhere to safety guidelines and contribute to the smooth operation of the charging infrastructure.

In Summary:

- Enhanced User Safety: Educational signage and training programs contribute to enhanced user safety by providing clear guidance on safety procedures, charging protocols, and emergency contacts.

- Reduced Misuse: Clear instructions from signage and user education programs reduce the risk of user error or misuse, preventing incidents that could impact the safety and functionality of the charging station.

- Optimized Station Utilization: Educated users are more likely to follow efficient charging practices, contributing to optimized station utilization and reduced waiting times for other users.

- User Empowerment: Training programs empower users with knowledge about available features and support, enabling them to navigate the charging process confidently and contribute to a positive user experience.

CHAPTER 06

BUSINESS MODELS AND REVENUE STREAMS

Business Models and Revenue Streams in the Charging Industry

1. Public Charging Stations:

- Accessibility and Convenience: Public charging stations cater to diverse users, providing convenient access for those without home charging options.

- Government Support: Explore the role of government initiatives in establishing and promoting public charging infrastructure.

2. Private Charging Infrastructure:

- Residential and Commercial Solutions: Investigate the development of private charging setups at homes and businesses, addressing the specific needs of individual users or organizations.

- Exclusive Networks: Explore the concept of private charging networks within gated communities or commercial complexes.

3. Workplace Charging Programs:

- Employee Satisfaction: Examine how workplace charging programs contribute to employee satisfaction, promoting sustainable practices within organizations.

- Business Benefits: Discuss the benefits for businesses in supporting EV adoption among employees.

4. Pricing Strategies:

- Per kWh Pricing: Analyze the per-kilowatt-hour pricing model, ensuring transparent billing based on actual energy consumption.

- Time-Based Pricing: Investigate time-based pricing, considering peak and off-peak rates to optimize costs for both users and providers.

- Flat Fee Models: Explore the simplicity and attractiveness of flat fee models for users.

5. Subscription and Membership Models:

- Subscription-Based Services: Assess the viability of subscription models, offering users consistent charging experiences for recurring fees.

- Membership Programs: Explore the benefits of membership programs, including user loyalty, perks, and sustainable revenue streams.

6. Sustainable Charging Business Practices:

- Green Charging Initiatives: Examine strategies for integrating renewable energy into charging infrastructure to promote environmental sustainability.

- Partnerships with Renewable Energy Providers: Explore collaborations with renewable energy providers to support eco-friendly charging practices.

7. Strategic Alliances in Charging Business:

- Automaker Collaborations: Investigate partnerships with automakers to advance electric vehicle adoption and improve charging infrastructure.

- Technology Integration: Explore the integration of smart grid connectivity and artificial intelligence to optimize charging operations.

8. Anticipating Future Trends:

- E-Mobility Trends: Discuss emerging trends in e-mobility, including advancements in battery technology and the rise of electric fleets.

- Regulatory Changes: Consider the impact of evolving regulations on safety standards, incentive programs, and environmental policies.

9. Maximizing Revenue Streams:

- Diversification Strategies: Explore revenue diversification through value-added services, local business partnerships, and advertising opportunities.

- Data Monetization: Discuss the potential for data monetization, leveraging user insights to create additional revenue streams.

This comprehensive exploration aims to guide industry stakeholders in understanding the various business models and revenue streams within the charging industry, emphasizing the importance of adaptability in a dynamic market.

1. Public Charging Stations:

- Overview: Public charging stations are accessible to all electric vehicle users, typically located in public areas such as parking lots, shopping centers, and along highways.

- Revenue Model: Public charging stations often operate on a pay-per-use model, charging users based on the amount of electricity consumed during the charging session.

2. Private Charging Infrastructure:

- Overview: Private charging infrastructure includes charging setups at residences, businesses, or private properties, catering to the charging needs of specific individuals or organizations.

- Revenue Model: In the case of residential setups, revenue may come from electricity fees. For businesses, it could be a combination of fees and employee benefits.

3. Workplace Charging Programs:

- Overview: Workplace charging programs involve the installation of charging stations at business premises to facilitate employees' electric vehicle charging needs.

- Revenue Model: The revenue model may involve employer-sponsored charging, providing a workplace benefit to employees, or a combination of employer and employee contributions.

These charging business models cater to different user needs and play essential roles in promoting the adoption of electric vehicles. Each model has its unique revenue streams and considerations, contributing to the overall growth of the charging infrastructure.

Public Charging Stations: Nurturing Accessibility and Sustainability
1. Overview of Public Charging Stations:

- Public charging stations are essential components of the electric vehicle (EV) infrastructure, providing convenient and accessible charging options for EV users who may not have access to home charging solutions.

2. Accessibility for Diverse Users:

- Urban Accessibility: Public charging stations are strategically placed in urban areas, offering easy access for residents without private charging options.

- Highway Infrastructure: Along highways, these stations play a crucial role in supporting long-distance travel for electric vehicles, reducing range anxiety for drivers.

3. Strategic Locations and Considerations:

- Commercial Centers: Stations are often located in shopping centers, business districts, and other high-traffic commercial areas to accommodate users while engaged in various activities.

- Public Parking Lots: Placing stations in public parking lots ensures EV users can conveniently charge their vehicles while running errands or attending events.

4. Role of Government Support:

- Incentives and Funding: Governments often provide incentives and funding to encourage the establishment of public charging infrastructure, promoting the adoption of electric vehicles.

- Regulatory Support: Government regulations may mandate or incentivize the inclusion of charging infrastructure in new developments or public spaces, contributing to the growth of public charging networks.

5. Enhancing Sustainability:

- Green Initiatives: Public charging stations can be integrated with green initiatives by incorporating renewable energy sources, aligning with sustainability goals.

- Collaboration with Energy Providers: Partnerships with energy providers may facilitate the use of clean and renewable energy, minimizing the environmental impact of charging operations.

6. User Experience and Connectivity:

- User-Friendly Interfaces: Public charging stations often feature user-friendly interfaces and payment systems to enhance the overall charging experience.

- Connectivity and Apps: Connectivity features and mobile apps provide users with real-time information on station availability, charging rates, and other relevant details.

7. Community Engagement:

- Awareness Programs: Governments and charging station operators may conduct awareness programs to educate communities about the benefits of electric vehicles and the availability of public charging options.

- Community Involvement: Involving local communities in the planning and placement of charging stations fosters a sense of ownership and support for sustainable transportation initiatives.

Public charging stations, strategically located and supported by government initiatives, play a vital role in creating a robust and accessible charging infrastructure. By fostering accessibility, sustainability, and community engagement, public charging stations contribute to the widespread adoption of electric vehicles.

Private Charging Infrastructure: Tailoring Solutions for Diverse Needs
1. Overview of Private Charging Infrastructure:

- Private charging infrastructure encompasses a range of solutions designed to meet the charging needs of electric vehicle (EV) users within specific residential or commercial settings, offering tailored and convenient options.

2. Residential Charging Setups:

- Home Charging Stations: Residential charging typically involves the installation of dedicated charging stations at users' homes, providing a convenient and private solution for overnight or daily charging.

- Charging Efficiency: Home setups allow EV owners to start each day with a fully charged vehicle, promoting a seamless and efficient charging routine.

3. Commercial and Residential Complexes:

- Exclusive Charging Networks: Some commercial or residential complexes offer exclusive charging networks, providing residents or employees with dedicated charging facilities.

- Community Integration: These setups contribute to community integration, fostering a sense of support for sustainable transportation within shared spaces.

4. Revenue Models for Private Charging:

- Residential Billing: In residential settings, revenue for charging infrastructure may come from electricity fees billed directly to residents.

- Commercial Partnerships: In commercial or residential complexes, revenue models may involve partnerships between property owners and charging station operators, potentially generating income through user fees or lease agreements.

5. Benefits of Private Charging Solutions:

- Convenience and Accessibility: Private charging setups offer users the convenience of charging within their own residences or workplace, minimizing the need for external charging trips.

- Parking Integration: Integration with parking facilities in commercial or residential complexes ensures that charging stations are easily accessible to users within the shared parking infrastructure.

6. Exclusive Charging Networks in Workplaces:

- Employee Benefits: Providing exclusive charging networks in workplace settings serves as a valuable employee benefit, contributing to employee satisfaction and supporting sustainable commuting practices.

- Employer Contributions: Employers may contribute to the infrastructure cost or offer charging as a subsidized benefit to employees, encouraging the adoption of electric vehicles.

7. Integration with Renewable Energy:

- Sustainable Practices: Private charging infrastructure may integrate with renewable energy sources, aligning with sustainability goals and reducing the carbon footprint associated with EV charging.

- Energy Efficiency: Utilizing clean energy sources enhances the overall environmental impact of private charging solutions.

8. Technological Advancements and Connectivity:

- Smart Charging Features: Private charging setups often incorporate smart charging features, allowing users to monitor and manage charging remotely through mobile apps or online platforms.

- Integration with Home Automation: Integration with home automation systems enhances the user experience, providing seamless control over charging operations.

Private charging infrastructure, whether at residences or within shared complexes, offers personalized solutions that cater to the specific needs of users. These setups contribute to the widespread adoption of electric vehicles by providing convenient, efficient, and community-integrated charging options.

Workplace Charging Programs: Empowering Employees and Sustainability
1. Overview of Workplace Charging Programs:

- Workplace charging programs involve the installation of electric vehicle (EV) charging stations at business premises, offering employees a convenient and accessible solution for charging their EVs while at work.

2. Employee Satisfaction and Retention:

- Employee Benefits: Workplace charging programs serve as a valuable employee benefit, enhancing job satisfaction and contributing to overall employee well-being.

- Attracting Talent: Companies offering EV charging as an employee benefit are more attractive to environmentally conscious job seekers.

3. Supporting Sustainable Commuting:

- Encouraging EV Adoption: Workplace charging programs encourage employees to consider electric vehicles by providing a reliable and accessible charging infrastructure.

- Reducing Carbon Footprint: Supporting sustainable commuting practices contributes to the reduction of the organization's carbon footprint and aligns with corporate social responsibility goals.

4. Corporate Image and Responsibility:

- Green Image: Employers with workplace charging programs enhance their corporate image as environmentally responsible organizations.

- Community Impact: Demonstrating commitment to sustainability positively impacts the organization's reputation within the local community.

5. Employee Productivity and Convenience:

- Reduced Range Anxiety: Employees with EVs experience reduced range anxiety, knowing they can conveniently charge their vehicles while at work.

- Time Savings: Workplace charging allows employees to maximize their time at the office, avoiding the need for additional charging stops during daily routines.

6. Cost-Effective Charging Solutions:

- Employer Contributions: Employers may choose to subsidize or contribute to the cost of workplace charging infrastructure, making it a cost-effective solution for employees.

- User Fees: Some workplace charging programs may involve user fees, providing a sustainable revenue stream for the organization.

7. Integration with Corporate Sustainability Goals:

- Environmental Stewardship: Workplace charging aligns with corporate sustainability goals, demonstrating a commitment to environmental stewardship.

- Emission Reduction: The adoption of electric vehicles through workplace charging contributes to reduced emissions, supporting broader environmental objectives.

8. Employee Engagement and Awareness:

- Awareness Programs: Organizations can conduct awareness programs to educate employees about the benefits of EVs and the workplace charging infrastructure.

- Employee Involvement: Involving employees in the decision-making process regarding charging infrastructure fosters a sense of involvement and support.

9. Government Incentives and Recognition:

- Incentives: Governments may provide incentives for organizations implementing workplace charging programs, such as tax credits or grants.

- Recognition: Organizations with workplace charging infrastructure may receive recognition for their contribution to sustainable transportation.

Workplace charging programs play a pivotal role in promoting sustainable commuting practices, enhancing employee satisfaction, and contributing to corporate sustainability initiatives. These programs are a strategic investment in both employee well-being and environmental responsibility.

Navigating Pricing Strategies for Sustainability and Profitability
1. Importance of Pricing Strategies:

- Balancing Sustainability and Profitability: Navigating pricing strategies is crucial to strike a balance between offering sustainable charging solutions and ensuring the financial viability of the electric vehicle (EV) charging business.

2. Pricing Strategies:

- Per kWh Pricing Model: Analyzing the per-kilowatt-hour (kWh) pricing model involves setting charges based on the amount of energy consumed during the charging session.

3. Per kWh Pricing Model: Advantages:

- Transparent Billing: Per kWh pricing provides transparent billing, ensuring that users pay for the actual energy consumed during the charging session.

- Cost Alignment: The model aligns costs directly with energy consumption, promoting fairness and accuracy in charging fees.

4. Considerations for Per kWh Pricing:

- Variable Charging Rates: Providers may implement variable charging rates, adjusting prices based on factors such as time of day, demand, or charging station location.

- Public Awareness: Communicating the per kWh pricing structure to users is essential to enhance understanding and build trust.

5. Benefits for Users:

- Cost Predictability: Per kWh pricing offers users cost predictability, allowing them to estimate charging expenses based on their vehicle's energy efficiency.

- Incentive for Efficiency: Users are encouraged to adopt more energy-efficient EVs and charging habits, aligning with sustainability goals.

6. Impact on Business Sustainability:

- Stable Revenue Streams: Per kWh pricing provides a stable revenue stream for charging providers, ensuring consistent income that supports the ongoing maintenance and expansion of charging infrastructure.

- User Trust: Transparent pricing builds user trust, fostering positive relationships and encouraging repeat business.

7. Aligning with Market Trends:

- Industry Standards: Aligning pricing strategies with industry standards ensures competitiveness and facilitates user acceptance.

- Flexibility: Businesses may adjust pricing strategies over time to adapt to market trends, technological advancements, and changes in consumer behavior.

8. Challenges and Mitigations:

- Regulatory Compliance: Charging providers must navigate regulatory considerations to ensure compliance with local laws and standards.

- User Education: Educating users about the per kWh pricing model helps mitigate challenges and enhances their understanding of the charging process.

Navigating pricing strategies, particularly through the per kWh pricing model, is a dynamic process that requires careful consideration of sustainability, user expectations, and business profitability. Striking the right balance contributes to the long-term success and impact of the EV charging business.

Time-Based Pricing: Optimizing Charging Costs for Users and Providers
1. Overview of Time-Based Pricing:

- Time-based pricing involves setting different charging rates based on the time of day, allowing electric vehicle (EV) charging providers to optimize costs and encourage users to charge during specific periods.

2. Peak and Off-Peak Rates:

- Peak Hours: Higher rates during peak hours incentivize users to avoid charging during periods of high demand, helping providers manage load distribution.

- Off-Peak Hours: Lower rates during off-peak hours encourage users to charge when demand is lower, maximizing the utilization of available infrastructure.

3. Advantages of Time-Based Pricing:

- Load Management: Time-based pricing helps distribute charging demand more evenly, reducing strain on the grid during peak hours.

- Cost Optimization: Users can optimize their charging costs by choosing to charge during off-peak hours, leading to potential cost savings.

4. User Considerations:

- Flexibility for Users: Time-based pricing provides users with flexibility to choose charging times that align with their preferences and cost-saving goals.

- Informed Decision-Making: Users can make informed decisions about when to charge based on real-time pricing information.

5. Benefits for Providers:

- Grid Stability: Managing charging demand through time-based pricing contributes to grid stability, reducing the risk of overloads during peak hours.

- Revenue Optimization: Providers can optimize revenue by encouraging users to charge during off-peak hours, maximizing the use of charging infrastructure.

6. Communication and Transparency:

- Clear Pricing Communication: Transparent communication about peak and off-peak rates is essential to ensure users understand the pricing structure.

- User Education: Educating users about the benefits of time-based pricing promotes understanding and encourages cooperation.

7. Integration with Smart Charging:

- Automated Rate Adjustments: Smart charging solutions can automate rate adjustments based on real-time grid demand, ensuring dynamic and responsive pricing.

- User-Friendly Interfaces: Implementing user-friendly interfaces and mobile apps helps users track and plan their charging sessions in accordance with time-based pricing.

8. Regulatory Compliance and Standards:

- Alignment with Regulations: Charging providers must align time-based pricing strategies with local regulations and industry standards.

- Consistency: Maintaining consistency in time-based pricing practices builds user trust and fosters a positive charging experience.

9. Balancing Profitability and User Incentives:

- Competitive Pricing: Providers must balance profitability with competitive pricing to attract users and encourage the adoption of electric vehicles.

- Rewarding Sustainable Behavior: Offering lower rates during off-peak hours rewards users for adopting sustainable charging habits.

Time-based pricing is a dynamic strategy that not only benefits charging providers by optimizing revenue but also empowers users to make informed choices that align with their preferences and cost-saving objectives. The successful implementation of time-based pricing requires clear communication, technological integration, and adherence to regulatory considerations.

Flat Fee Models: Simplicity and Revenue Stability
1. Overview of Flat Fee Models:

- Flat fee models involve charging users a fixed amount for each charging session, providing simplicity and predictability in pricing.

2. Simplicity and User Appeal:

- Easy Understanding: Flat fee models are straightforward for users to understand, eliminating the complexity associated with variable pricing structures.

- Predictable Costs: Users appreciate the predictability of charging costs, as they pay the same amount regardless of the duration or energy consumed during the session.

3. Single-Charge Convenience:

- No Time-Based Considerations: Users are not concerned with time-of-day considerations or peak/off-peak rates, simplifying the charging experience.

- Convenient Billing: Flat fee models result in a single charge for each session, streamlining the billing process for both users and providers.

4. User Flexibility:

- Freedom to Charge Anytime: Users have the flexibility to charge their vehicles at any time without worrying about fluctuations in pricing based on time of day.

- No Need for Rate Monitoring: Users can avoid monitoring rates or adjusting their charging habits based on varying pricing structures.

5. Attractiveness for Occasional Users:

- Intermittent Users: Flat fee models are appealing to occasional users who may not charge frequently, as they don't need to track charging patterns or consider time-based rates.

- Visitor-Friendly: Charging stations with flat fee models are visitor-friendly, as guests can easily understand and pay a fixed amount for their charging session.

6. Revenue Stability for Providers:

- Predictable Income: Providers benefit from revenue stability, as each charging session generates a consistent income irrespective of usage patterns.

- Simplified Operations: Billing processes are simplified, reducing administrative complexities associated with variable-rate structures.

7. Challenges and Considerations:

- Variable Costs: While users appreciate predictability, flat fee models may not account for variable costs such as electricity rates or maintenance expenses.

- Balancing Profitability: Providers must set flat fees at a level that ensures profitability while remaining attractive to users.

8. Competitive Positioning:

- Market Differentiation: Providers may use flat fee models for market differentiation, offering a simple and user-friendly alternative to competitors with more complex pricing structures.

- Targeting Specific User Segments: Flat fee models can be targeted toward specific user segments, such as occasional users or those who prioritize simplicity.

9. Transparency and Communication:

- Clear Communication: Transparent communication about flat fee structures is essential to build user trust and avoid misunderstandings.

- Educating Users: Providers may need to educate users about the benefits of flat fee models and how they contribute to a seamless charging experience.

Flat fee models, with their simplicity and predictability, offer an attractive option for users seeking an uncomplicated charging experience. While they simplify operations for providers, careful consideration is needed to ensure a balance between user appeal and revenue stability.

Subscription and Membership Models: Enhancing User Experience through Consistency

1. Introduction to Subscription and Membership Models:

- Subscription and membership models involve users paying a recurring fee for access to charging services, providing a consistent and potentially cost-effective experience.

2. Subscription-Based Services:

- Recurring Fee Structure: Users subscribe to a service for a regular fee, gaining access to specific benefits, such as discounted charging rates or exclusive features.

- Predictable Costs: Subscribers benefit from predictable charging costs, fostering loyalty and commitment to the service.

3. Benefits for Users:

- Cost Predictability: Subscribers enjoy the predictability of charging costs, often receiving discounted rates compared to non-subscribers.

- Access to Exclusive Features: Some subscription models offer additional perks, such as priority access to charging stations or special promotions, enhancing the overall user experience.

4. Flexibility in Subscription Tiers:

- Tiered Subscriptions: Providers can offer tiered subscription models with different levels of benefits, catering to diverse user preferences and charging needs.

- Customization: Users can choose a subscription tier that aligns with their usage patterns, optimizing the value they receive from the service.

5. Revenue Stability for Providers:

- Consistent Income: Subscription models contribute to revenue stability, ensuring a consistent income stream for charging providers.

- Enhanced Financial Planning: Predictable subscriber numbers facilitate financial planning and infrastructure maintenance.

6. Accessibility and Inclusivity:

- Affordability: Subscription models can make EV charging more affordable for users who charge frequently, encouraging the adoption of electric vehicles.

- Inclusivity: Offering subscription options alongside other pricing models ensures accessibility for users with varying preferences.

7. Challenges and Considerations:

- User Perceived Value: Providers must offer sufficient value in subscription packages to justify the recurring fee and retain subscribers.

- Balancing Benefits: Striking the right balance between subscriber benefits and profitability is essential for the long-term sustainability of subscription models.

8. Technology Integration and User Experience:

- Mobile App Integration: Seamless integration with mobile apps enhances the user experience, allowing subscribers to easily access benefits and manage their subscription.

- User-Friendly Interfaces: Intuitive interfaces contribute to positive user experiences, encouraging long-term engagement with the subscription service.

9. Communication and Marketing:

-       Clear   Communication: Transparent communication about subscription benefits and costs is crucial to attract and retain subscribers.

- Marketing Strategies: Effective marketing strategies can highlight the value proposition of subscription models, enticing users to subscribe and experience the benefits.

10. Adapting to User Feedback:

- Feedback Mechanisms: Providers should establish feedback mechanisms to understand subscriber needs and preferences, allowing for continuous improvement of the subscription offering.

- Adaptive Models: Subscription models may evolve based on user feedback and changing market dynamics to stay competitive and relevant.

Subscription and membership models offer a balance between user benefits and revenue stability, creating a mutually beneficial relationship between charging providers and users. By enhancing the predictability of charging costs and providing additional perks, subscription models contribute to a positive and consistent charging experience.

Membership Programs: Fostering Loyalty and Sustainable Revenue
1. Introduction to Membership Programs:

- Membership programs involve users paying a periodic fee for exclusive access to charging benefits, fostering loyalty and creating a sustainable revenue stream for charging providers.

2. Building User Loyalty:

- Member-Exclusive Benefits: Membership programs offer exclusive benefits such as discounted rates, priority access to charging stations, and additional perks, encouraging users to commit to the service.

- Long-Term Relationships: By providing added value to members, charging providers cultivate long-term relationships, contributing to user loyalty and retention.

3. Perks and Incentives:

- Discounted Charging Rates: Members may enjoy discounted rates per kWh, creating a cost-effective solution for frequent users.

- Priority Access: Membership programs may grant priority access to charging stations during peak hours, ensuring members have a seamless charging experience.

4. Sustainable Revenue Stream:

- Predictable Income: Membership fees contribute to a consistent and predictable revenue stream for charging providers, aiding in financial planning and infrastructure development.

- Membership Renewals: Providers benefit from recurring membership renewals, creating an ongoing source of income.

5. Tiered Membership Levels:

- Diverse Benefits: Providers can offer tiered membership levels with varying benefits, catering to different user preferences and charging needs.

- Customization: Users can choose a membership tier that aligns with their usage patterns and desired perks, enhancing the overall membership experience.

6. Community Engagement:

- Member Events and Promotions: Membership programs provide opportunities for exclusive events, promotions, or collaborations, fostering a sense of community among members.

- Feedback Channels: Establishing feedback channels within membership programs allows providers to adapt offerings based on member preferences.

7. Technology Integration:

- Mobile App Features: Integration with mobile apps enhances the user experience, allowing members to easily access and redeem exclusive benefits.

- Member-Only Platforms: Consider creating member-only platforms or sections within apps for a personalized and enhanced user experience.

8. Communication and Transparency:

- Clear Benefit Communication: Transparent communication about membership benefits, renewal processes, and any changes in offerings is crucial to maintaining trust.

- Regular Updates: Regular updates on upcoming perks, events, or improvements in the charging infrastructure keep members engaged and informed.

9. Inclusivity and Accessibility:

- Balancing Exclusive and Inclusive Features: While providing exclusive benefits, membership programs should remain inclusive to accommodate a broad range of users.

- Affordable Options: Offering different membership price points ensures accessibility, allowing users with varying budgets to participate.

10. Promotional Strategies:

- Launch Promotions: Attract initial members by offering special promotions or discounts during the launch of the membership program.

- Referral Programs: Encourage member referrals through incentive programs, expanding the reach of the membership community.

Membership programs, with their focus on user loyalty and sustainable revenue, offer a strategic approach for charging providers to create a dedicated user base. By providing valuable perks and fostering community engagement, membership programs contribute to a positive and enduring relationship between charging providers and their members.

Aligning Business Models with Market Needs and Sustainability Goals
1. Understanding Market Needs:

- Conduct thorough market research to identify the specific needs and preferences of the target audience, considering factors such as charging frequency, user demographics, and regional variations.

2. Public Charging Stations:

- Market Need: For urban and high-traffic areas with diverse users.

- Business Model: Implement a mix of flat fee and time-based pricing to accommodate different user preferences, ensuring accessibility for occasional users and those seeking simplicity.

3. Private Charging Infrastructure:

- Market Need: Catering to residential and exclusive settings.

- Business Model: Subscription-based services can offer convenience and cost predictability for residents or members of private communities, fostering loyalty.

4. Workplace Charging Programs:

- Market Need: Addressing the charging needs of employees during work hours.

- Business Model: Introduce workplace-focused subscription or membership models, providing tailored benefits like discounted rates and priority access to charging stations.

5. Balancing Profitability and Affordability:

- Market Need: Ensuring competitive pricing while maintaining profitability.

- Business Model: Employ tiered subscription models, offering different levels of benefits to accommodate various user segments and usage patterns.

6. Environmental Considerations:

- Market Need: Catering to environmentally conscious users.

- Business Model: Highlight sustainability in marketing and incorporate eco-friendly features. Consider membership programs with exclusive benefits for users committed to sustainable practices.

7. Technology Integration for User Experience:

- Market Need: Providing a seamless and user-friendly charging experience.

- Business Model: Invest in smart charging solutions and mobile app integration. Subscription and membership models can include technology-driven perks for enhanced user convenience.

8. Regulatory Compliance:

- Market Need: Adhering to local regulations and standards.

- Business Model: Ensure that pricing models align with regulatory requirements. Collaborate with government entities for public charging stations to streamline compliance.

9. Financial Incentives and Public-Private Partnerships:

- Market Need: Leveraging financial incentives and collaborations for infrastructure development.

- Business Model: Explore partnerships with governments for public charging stations, taking advantage of incentives. Private charging infrastructure can be funded through a mix of private investments and government grants.

10. Long-Term Sustainability:

- Market Need: Ensuring the viability of the business model over the long term.

- Business Model: Incorporate ROI analyses into decision-making. Subscription and membership models contribute to long-term sustainability by fostering user loyalty and providing a consistent revenue stream.

11. Adaptability to Market Trends:

- Market Need: Staying relevant in a dynamic market.

- Business Model: Regularly assess market trends and adapt business models accordingly. Flexible pricing structures and innovative features within subscription or membership programs support adaptability.

By aligning business models with market needs and sustainability goals, charging providers can not only meet the diverse requirements of users but also contribute to the long-term success of the electric vehicle charging business. Understanding the market landscape and incorporating sustainable practices ensure a strategic and responsible approach to business development.

Sustainable Charging Business Practices: Green Charging Initiatives and Collaborations with Renewable Energy Providers

1. Green Charging Initiatives:

- Integration of Renewable Energy:

- Utilize solar panels, wind turbines, or other renewable energy sources to power charging stations.

- Implement energy storage solutions to store excess energy for use during periods of low renewable energy production.

- Energy-Efficient Charging Infrastructure:

- Invest in energy-efficient charging equipment to minimize energy consumption.

- Explore smart charging technologies that optimize energy usage based on grid demand and renewable energy availability.

- Carbon Offset Programs:

- Implement carbon offset programs to neutralize the environmental impact of charging operations.

- Collaborate with environmental organizations to support projects that reduce or capture carbon emissions.

2. Collaborations with Renewable Energy Providers:

- Procuring Renewable Energy:

- Collaborate with renewable energy providers to procure clean energy for charging operations.

- Establish power purchase agreements (PPAs) to ensure a consistent supply of renewable energy.

- Marketing Green Credentials:

- Showcase the use of renewable energy in marketing materials to build a green image.

- Highlight environmental initiatives to attract environmentally conscious users.

- Educational Campaigns:

- Conduct educational campaigns to inform users about the positive environmental impact of utilizing renewable energy for charging.

- Emphasize the reduction of carbon footprint and the promotion of sustainable transportation.

- Incentivizing Renewable Energy Adoption:

- Offer incentives for renewable energy adoption, encouraging users to choose green energy options for charging.

- Collaborate with utility companies to promote renewable energy programs for electric vehicle users.

3. Benefits of Collaborations:

- Enhanced Sustainability Image:

- Collaborating with renewable energy providers enhances the sustainability image of the charging business.

- Attracts environmentally conscious users who prioritize eco-friendly charging options.

- Stable Energy Costs:

- Partnering with renewable energy providers can provide stability in energy costs, contributing to long-term financial sustainability.

- Mitigates risks associated with fluctuating electricity prices.

- Regulatory Compliance:

- Ensures compliance with environmental regulations and standards by incorporating renewable energy sources.

- Positions the charging business as a responsible and compliant player in the green energy sector.

- Community Engagement:

- Engages the local community in green initiatives, fostering a positive relationship with residents and businesses.

- Collaborations with renewable energy providers can result in joint community outreach programs.

- Support for Renewable Energy Transition:

- Demonstrates support for the transition to a renewable energy future, aligning the charging business with broader sustainability goals.

- Contributes to the overall growth of the renewable energy sector.

By implementing green charging initiatives and collaborating with renewable energy providers, charging businesses can actively contribute to environmental sustainability, reduce their carbon footprint, and appeal to a growing market of eco-conscious electric vehicle users.

Strategic Alliances and Future Trends in Electric Vehicle Charging Business
1. Strategic Alliances:

- Automaker Partnerships:

    - Collaborate with automakers to integrate charging solutions into new vehicle models.

    - Explore joint marketing initiatives to promote both electric vehicles and charging infrastructure.

- Energy Company Collaborations:

    - Form partnerships with energy companies for shared resources and expertise.

    - Collaborate on the development of innovative charging technologies and grid integration.

- Tech Firm Collaborations:

    - Partner with technology firms to enhance user interfaces, mobile apps, and smart charging capabilities.

    - Explore joint ventures for the development of advanced charging technologies.

- Public-Private Partnerships:

 - Engage in public-private partnerships with governments to expand charging infrastructure.

 - Leverage government support for regulatory compliance and infrastructure development.

2. Future Trends:

- Battery Technology Advancements:

 - Stay abreast of developments in battery technology to support faster charging, longer range, and increased energy density.

 - Explore partnerships with companies involved in battery research and development.

- Automated Charging Solutions:

 - Anticipate the rise of automated charging solutions, including robotic systems for plug-in and wireless charging.

 - Collaborate with technology companies to integrate automation into charging infrastructure.

- Vehicle-to-Grid (V2G) Integration:

 - Explore V2G capabilities, allowing electric vehicles to contribute back to the grid during peak demand.

- Collaborate with energy companies to implement V2G solutions and optimize grid stability.

- Charging Infrastructure in Urban Planning:

- Collaborate with city planners to integrate charging infrastructure into urban development projects.

- Anticipate and adapt to the growing need for charging stations in urban areas.

- Integration with Renewable Energy:

- Strengthen collaborations with renewable energy providers to align with sustainable energy trends.

- Explore options for on-site renewable energy generation at charging stations.

- Blockchain and Smart Contracts:

- Investigate the potential use of blockchain technology and smart contracts for secure and transparent billing.

- Collaborate with technology firms to implement blockchain solutions in charging operations.

- Enhanced User Experience:

- Invest in technologies that enhance the overall user experience, including seamless payment systems, real-time data analytics, and personalized charging preferences.

- Collaborate with tech companies to develop user-friendly interfaces and mobile app features.

- Global Interoperability Standards:

- Support the development and adoption of global interoperability standards for charging connectors and communication protocols.

- Collaborate with industry stakeholders to ensure compatibility and ease of use for electric vehicle users worldwide.

- Innovative Business Models:

- Stay agile in adapting business models to evolving market trends.

- Collaborate with industry leaders and startups to explore and implement innovative pricing and service models.

Strategic alliances and a focus on future trends position electric vehicle charging businesses to navigate the dynamic landscape of the industry, fostering innovation, sustainability, and a seamless user experience.

Importance of Strategic Alliances in Charging Business

1. Collaborations with Automakers:

- Promoting Electric Vehicle Adoption:

- Collaborating with automakers creates a symbiotic relationship by promoting electric vehicle adoption alongside charging infrastructure development.

- Automaker partnerships can include joint marketing campaigns, offering bundled services to incentivize consumers.

- Synergies in Technology Development:

- Collaborations provide opportunities for joint research and development in charging technologies, optimizing compatibility and efficiency.

- Automaker input ensures that charging infrastructure aligns with the evolving needs and specifications of electric vehicle models.

- Seamless User Experience:

- Integrating charging solutions with automaker systems enhances the overall user experience, making charging more convenient and user-friendly.

- Collaborative efforts can lead to standardized interfaces and interoperability, simplifying the charging process for consumers.

- Increased Visibility and Credibility:

- Partnering with reputable automakers enhances the visibility and credibility of charging businesses.

- Automaker endorsements contribute to consumer trust, driving increased usage of associated charging infrastructure.

2. Importance of Technology Integration:

- Optimizing Charging Operations:

- Integrating emerging technologies, such as smart grid connectivity and artificial intelligence, optimizes charging station operations.

- Smart technologies allow for real-time data analysis, predictive maintenance, and dynamic adjustments to charging parameters.

- Enhanced User Experience:

- Technology integration enhances user experiences through features like mobile apps, remote monitoring, and personalized charging preferences.

- Artificial intelligence can anticipate user behavior and optimize charging sessions for efficiency and cost-effectiveness.

- Efficient Energy Management:

- Smart grid connectivity enables charging stations to communicate with the grid, contributing to efficient energy management.

- Load balancing and demand response capabilities help prevent grid congestion and reduce electricity costs.

- Future-Proofing Infrastructure:

    - Integrating advanced technologies future-proofs charging infrastructure, ensuring compatibility with evolving industry standards.

    - Collaborating with tech firms allows charging businesses to stay ahead of technological advancements.

- Sustainability and Environmental Impact:

    - Technology integration can include features that prioritize renewable energy use, reducing the environmental impact of charging operations.

    - Smart technologies contribute to energy efficiency, aligning with sustainability goals.

- Operational Efficiency and Cost Savings:

    - Technology-driven solutions streamline operational processes, reducing maintenance costs and improving overall efficiency.

    - Predictive analytics and remote monitoring help identify and address issues before they impact charging station performance.

Collaborations with automakers and the integration of advanced technologies are crucial for charging businesses to thrive in a rapidly evolving industry. These strategic alliances contribute to user satisfaction, operational efficiency, and the overall growth of the electric vehicle ecosystem.

Anticipating Future Trends and Evolving Market Dynamics

1. Continuous Market Research:

- Importance: Regularly conduct market research to identify emerging trends, changing consumer preferences, and technological advancements.

- Action Steps:

- Engage in surveys, interviews, and industry reports to stay informed about evolving market dynamics.

- Monitor competitors and analyze their strategies to adapt to changing market trends.

2. Partnerships with Innovators:

- Importance: Collaborate with startups, research institutions, and tech innovators to stay at the forefront of new technologies and business models.

- Action Steps:

- Foster partnerships with organizations specializing in electric vehicle technologies, renewable energy, and smart grid solutions.

- Participate in innovation hubs or accelerators to access cutting-edge developments.

3. Adaptability in Business Models:

- Importance: Be agile and ready to adjust business models based on market shifts, regulatory changes, and technological advancements.

- Action Steps:

- Regularly review and update business models to align with emerging trends.

- Embrace flexibility in pricing structures and service offerings.

4. Global Interoperability Standards:

- Importance: Support and contribute to the development of global interoperability standards for charging connectors and communication protocols.

- Action Steps:

- Engage with industry associations and regulatory bodies to stay informed about evolving standards.

- Collaborate with stakeholders to establish consistent and user-friendly charging experiences globally.

5. Diversification of Services:

- Importance: Explore additional services beyond traditional charging, such as energy storage solutions, vehicle-to-grid integration, and value-added offerings.

- Action Steps:

- Conduct feasibility studies on diversification opportunities.

- Assess user needs and market demand for complementary services.

6. User Education and Engagement:

- Importance: Proactively educate users about advancements in charging technologies, environmental benefits, and the evolving electric vehicle landscape.

- Action Steps:

- Implement user engagement programs, webinars, and educational campaigns.

- Utilize social media and digital platforms to share relevant information with the user community.

7. Regulatory Landscape Monitoring:

- Importance: Stay informed about regulatory changes and policy developments related to electric vehicles, charging infrastructure, and environmental standards.

- Action Steps:

- Establish a regulatory monitoring team to track legislative updates.

- Engage in advocacy efforts to influence supportive policies and regulations.

8. Integration with Smart Cities:

- Importance: Anticipate the integration of charging infrastructure into smart city initiatives and urban planning.

- Action Steps:

- Collaborate with city planners, municipalities, and urban development projects.

- Participate in discussions on incorporating charging solutions into smart city frameworks.

9. Collaborations for Research and Development:

- Importance: Engage in collaborative research and development projects to contribute to technological innovations and stay ahead of market trends.

- Action Steps:

- Partner with research institutions, universities, and industry experts on projects related to charging technology advancements.

- Leverage collective knowledge to drive industry innovation.

10. Environmental Sustainability Commitment:

- Importance: Demonstrate a strong commitment to environmental sustainability, aligning business practices with global efforts to combat climate change.

- Action Steps:

- Implement green charging initiatives, such as renewable energy integration and carbon offset programs.

- Communicate sustainability efforts transparently to users and stakeholders.

Anticipating future trends and evolving market dynamics requires a proactive and adaptive approach. By staying informed, fostering strategic partnerships, and embracing innovation, charging businesses can position themselves as leaders in the dynamic electric vehicle ecosystem.

Importance of Anticipating Future Trends:

1. Strategic Planning:

- Importance: Anticipating future trends allows businesses to strategically plan for upcoming changes in the market.

- Benefits: Helps in resource allocation, technology adoption, and the development of innovative solutions ahead of competitors.

2. Competitive Advantage:

- Importance: Staying ahead of emerging trends provides a competitive advantage in a rapidly evolving industry.

- Benefits: Positions the business as an industry leader, attracting customers and partners seeking cutting-edge solutions.

3. Innovation and Adaptation:

- Importance: Awareness of future trends fosters a culture of innovation and adaptability within the organization.

- Benefits: Enables the business to quickly pivot and adopt new technologies, ensuring relevance in a dynamic market.

4. Customer Satisfaction:

- Importance: Meeting or exceeding evolving customer expectations requires understanding and adapting to emerging trends.

- Benefits: Enhances customer satisfaction by providing services aligned with the latest technologies and industry advancements.

5. Risk Mitigation:

- Importance: Anticipating trends helps identify potential risks and challenges early on.

- Benefits: Allows businesses to proactively mitigate risks, reducing the impact of unexpected market shifts.

6. Long-Term Sustainability:

- Importance: Planning for future trends contributes to the long-term sustainability of the business.

- Benefits: Positions the business to navigate changing market dynamics and remain relevant over an extended period.

E-Mobility Trends:

1. Advancements in Battery Technology:

- Impact on Charging Infrastructure: Faster-charging capabilities, increased energy density, and longer-range batteries influence the design and capabilities of charging stations.

2. Rise of Electric Fleets:

- Impact on Charging Infrastructure: Growing electric fleets necessitate the development of dedicated charging solutions tailored to fleet management needs.

3. Integration with Smart Cities:

- Impact on Charging Infrastructure: Charging infrastructure becomes an integral part of smart city initiatives, with enhanced connectivity, data analytics, and integration into urban planning.

4. Vehicle-to-Grid (V2G) Technology:

- Impact on Charging Infrastructure: V2G integration influences the design of charging stations to support bidirectional energy flow and grid stabilization.

Regulatory Changes:

1. Safety Standards and Certifications:

- Influence on Charging Business: Evolving safety standards impact the design, installation, and operation of charging infrastructure, ensuring compliance with industry regulations.

2. Incentive Programs:

- Influence on Charging Business: Changes in incentive programs can drive shifts in consumer behavior and impact the utilization of charging stations.

3. Environmental Policies:

- Influence on Charging Business: Stringent environmental policies may drive the adoption of green charging initiatives, emphasizing renewable energy sources and reduced carbon emissions.

4. Accessibility and Inclusivity Regulations:

- Influence on Charging Business: Regulations promoting accessibility and inclusivity impact the design and features of charging stations to accommodate users of varying abilities.

5. Emission Standards:

- Influence on Charging Business: Evolving emission standards can drive increased adoption of electric vehicles, influencing the demand for charging infrastructure.

Anticipating e-mobility trends and regulatory changes ensures that charging businesses are well-prepared for the future, enabling strategic decisions and sustainable growth in the dynamic electric vehicle ecosystem.

Importance of Maximizing Revenue Streams in a Dynamic Industry:

1. Adaptation to Market Changes:

- Importance: Maximizing revenue streams enables businesses to adapt to changes in the dynamic industry landscape.

- Benefits: Ensures financial resilience by diversifying income sources and mitigating risks associated with market fluctuations.

2. Sustainable Growth:

- Importance: A diverse revenue portfolio contributes to sustainable long-term growth.

- Benefits: Allows businesses to withstand industry shifts and economic uncertainties, fostering stability and resilience.

3. Competitive Edge:

- Importance: Businesses with multiple revenue streams gain a competitive edge in a rapidly evolving market.

- Benefits: Positions the business as versatile and adaptable, attracting customers and partners seeking comprehensive solutions.

4. Innovation and Agility:

- Importance: Exploring new revenue streams encourages innovation and agility within the organization.

- Benefits: Fosters a culture of continuous improvement, ensuring the business remains at the forefront of industry trends.

5. Enhanced Financial Performance:

- Importance: Maximizing revenue streams contributes to enhanced financial performance and profitability.

- Benefits: Provides financial flexibility to invest in technology upgrades, expansion, and the development of new services.

6. Resilience Against Disruptions:

- Importance: Diversifying revenue sources enhances resilience against unexpected disruptions, such as economic downturns or changes in consumer behavior.

- Benefits: Helps businesses weather challenges by reducing dependence on a single income stream.

Maximizing Revenue Streams:

1. Diversification Strategies:

- Exploration of Avenues: Explore various avenues for revenue diversification, including:

- Value-Added Services: Offer services beyond charging, such as premium memberships, convenience features, or exclusive partnerships with local businesses.

- Local Business Partnerships: Collaborate with local businesses for mutually beneficial partnerships, such as cross-promotions or co-branded offerings.

- Advertising Opportunities: Utilize charging stations as advertising spaces, generating revenue through partnerships with brands.

2. Data Monetization:

- Potential for Revenue Generation: Discuss the potential for data monetization by leveraging user insights and charging patterns.

- User Insights: Analyze anonymized user data to extract valuable insights, providing targeted information for businesses or city planners.

- Charging Patterns: Offer anonymized charging pattern data to energy providers, urban planners, or researchers, creating an additional revenue stream.

3. Strategic Partnerships:

- Exploration of Collaborations: Explore strategic partnerships with entities in related industries to expand revenue opportunities.

- Energy Companies: Collaborate with energy companies for joint ventures, such as shared infrastructure or combined service offerings.

- Automakers: Explore partnerships with automakers for joint marketing campaigns, exclusive benefits, or bundled services.

4. Subscription Models:

- Introduction of Subscription Plans: Introduce subscription models to offer users consistent charging experiences for a recurring fee.

- Tiered Plans: Develop tiered subscription plans with varying levels of benefits, appealing to a diverse user base.

5. Value-Added Services:

- Introduction of Additional Services: Offer value-added services to enhance user experiences and create additional revenue streams.

- Charging Station Amenities: Provide amenities such as convenience stores, cafes, or rest areas at charging locations to attract users.

Maximizing revenue streams ensures the financial sustainability and adaptability of charging businesses in a dynamic industry, fostering innovation and resilience against market uncertainties.

Conclusion: Striking the Balance and Adapting to Change

In the dynamic landscape of the electric vehicle (EV) charging business, striking the delicate balance between accessibility, sustainability, and profitability emerges as a paramount consideration. The journey explored the multifaceted aspects of building and managing an EV charging business, unraveling the interconnected threads that define success in this burgeoning industry.

Balancing Accessibility, Sustainability, and Profitability:

As we conclude, it is evident that accessibility, ensuring widespread availability and user-friendly experiences, lays the foundation for widespread EV adoption. Simultaneously, sustainability becomes the cornerstone, integrating eco-friendly practices and renewable energy solutions to align with global environmental goals. Crucially, amidst these considerations, profitability remains essential, driving financial sustainability and enabling continuous innovation.

Adaptability in the Evolving Landscape:

The dynamic nature of the electric vehicle landscape necessitates a commitment to adaptability. From technological advancements to regulatory shifts, staying informed about industry trends and being ready to pivot is imperative. The journey through this exploration highlighted the importance of anticipating future trends, fostering innovation, and strategically planning for sustained growth.

Looking Forward:

As the electric vehicle revolution accelerates, the role of EV charging businesses becomes increasingly pivotal. From the historic roots of electric propulsion to the intricacies of charging technology, environmental benefits, and market dynamics, this journey aimed to equip stakeholders with comprehensive insights.

In conclusion, the success of an EV charging business lies not just in the electrons it delivers but in its ability to harmonize accessibility, sustainability, and profitability. As the charging infrastructure continues to evolve, businesses that embrace change, seize opportunities, and contribute to the broader goals of a sustainable future are poised to thrive in this electrifying journey. The road ahead is charged with potential, and the journey has just begun.

CHAPTER 07

OPERATING AND MANAGING CHARGING STATIONS

Section 7.1: Maintenance and Upkeep

What is Maintenance and Upkeep?

Maintenance and upkeep refer to the regular care, inspections, and technical measures undertaken to ensure the optimal functioning, safety, and longevity of electric vehicle (EV) charging stations.

Importance:

1. Optimal Performance:

- Regular maintenance guarantees that charging stations operate at peak performance, delivering efficient and reliable services to users.

2. User Safety:

- Ensuring infrastructure integrity through upkeep contributes to user safety, preventing potential hazards and accidents.

3. Reliability:

- Technical maintenance, including software updates and hardware checks, enhances the reliability of charging stations, reducing downtime and user inconvenience.

4. Cost-Efficiency:

- Proactive maintenance can prevent major issues, reducing the overall operational costs associated with extensive repairs or replacements.

5. User Experience:

- Well-maintained stations contribute to a positive user experience, fostering trust and confidence among EV drivers.

6. Longevity of Infrastructure:

- Upkeep measures extend the lifespan of charging infrastructure, maximizing the return on investment for businesses and stakeholders.

7. Remote Monitoring:

- Utilizing remote monitoring systems allows for real-time tracking, enabling proactive identification and resolution of potential issues.

In essence, maintenance and upkeep are imperative for sustaining the reliability, safety, and efficiency of EV charging stations, ultimately contributing to the success of the charging infrastructure and the satisfaction of its users.

Routine Inspections: Ensuring Optimal Performance

Routine inspections form a foundational practice in the maintenance and upkeep of electric vehicle (EV) charging stations. These inspections involve systematically checking the charging equipment at regular intervals to:

1. Ensure Optimal Performance:

- By conducting routine inspections, charging station operators can verify that each component, from cables to connectors, is functioning at its best.

2. Identify Potential Issues Promptly:

- Early detection of wear and tear, loose connections, or any signs of malfunction allows for prompt intervention, preventing minor issues from escalating into major problems.

3. Enhance User Safety:

- Regular examinations contribute to user safety by identifying and rectifying any potential safety hazards, ensuring that EV drivers can trust the reliability of the charging infrastructure.

4. Minimize Downtime:

- Proactive identification of issues minimizes downtime for the charging station. Addressing potential problems swiftly contributes to the overall efficiency and availability of the station.

5. Extend Equipment Lifespan:

- Consistent inspections and timely maintenance contribute to the longevity of charging equipment, protecting the investment made in the infrastructure.

6. Compliance with Standards:

- Routine inspections help ensure that the charging station remains in compliance with safety and regulatory standards, meeting the necessary requirements for operation.

7. Remote Monitoring Integration:

- Integrating remote monitoring systems enhances routine inspections by providing real-time data on station performance, allowing operators to assess the status of multiple stations without physical presence.

In summary, routine inspections are a proactive measure that safeguards the optimal functioning of EV charging stations, addressing issues promptly and contributing to the overall reliability and safety of the infrastructure.

Technical Maintenance: Ensuring Cutting-Edge Efficiency

Technical maintenance involves a comprehensive approach to keep electric vehicle (EV) charging stations up-to-date and operating at peak efficiency. This encompasses both software and hardware aspects to ensure the continued functionality and innovation of the charging infrastructure:

1. Software Updates:

- Regularly updating charging station software is crucial for incorporating the latest features, security patches, and performance enhancements. This ensures that stations remain compatible with evolving industry standards and user expectations.

2. Firmware Upgrades:

- Updating firmware is essential for addressing any bugs or glitches, improving the overall stability and reliability of the charging station's internal systems.

3. Security Patching:

- Implementing security updates protects against potential vulnerabilities, safeguarding user data and the integrity of the charging station's operation.

4. Compatibility Checks:

- Technical maintenance involves assessing the compatibility of the charging station with various electric vehicle models and adapting software to accommodate new connectors or communication protocols.

5. Hardware Checks:

- Routine hardware inspections verify the physical components of the charging station, including cables, connectors, and internal mechanisms. This helps identify wear and tear or potential issues that may affect performance.

6. Performance Optimization:

- Adjusting charging parameters and optimizing performance settings contribute to efficient energy transfer, reducing charging times, and enhancing the overall user experience.

7. Integration with Smart Technologies:

- Technical maintenance may involve integrating the charging station with smart technologies, such as IoT devices or grid connectivity, to enable advanced functionalities like remote monitoring and demand response capabilities.

8. User Interface Enhancements:

- Improving the user interface through technical updates ensures a seamless and user-friendly experience, contributing to user satisfaction and ease of operation.

By conducting thorough technical maintenance, charging station operators can stay at the forefront of innovation, providing users with cutting-edge services while maintaining the reliability and security of the charging infrastructure.

Infrastructure Integrity: Safeguarding Charging Station Assets

Ensuring the integrity of the charging station infrastructure is a fundamental aspect of maintenance, addressing various factors to guarantee safe and reliable operation:

1. Wear and Tear Mitigation:

- Regularly inspecting physical components, such as cables, plugs, and connectors, helps identify signs of wear and tear. Timely replacements or repairs prevent operational issues and maintain user safety.

2. Weather-Related Damage Prevention:

- Shielding charging stations from adverse weather conditions is essential. Implement protective measures, such as weatherproof enclosures or shelters, to prevent damage caused by rain, snow, extreme temperatures, or other environmental factors.

3. Structural Examination:

- Periodic structural inspections ensure that the charging station's mounting, foundation, and overall physical integrity remain intact. This helps prevent potential hazards and maintains the station's stability.

4. Safety Hazard Identification:

- Thorough assessments identify potential safety hazards, including exposed wiring, damaged insulation, or compromised structural elements. Addressing these concerns promptly is crucial for user safety.

5. Regular Cleaning and Maintenance:

- Keep the charging station clean from debris, dust, and contaminants that may affect its performance. Regular cleaning ensures the visibility of safety signage and maintains a positive user experience.

6. Accessibility Considerations:

- Ensure that the charging station remains accessible to users, addressing any obstacles or challenges that may arise over time. Accessibility is essential for a user-friendly experience and compliance with regulations.

7. Surge Protection:

- Implement surge protection measures to safeguard charging station components from power fluctuations, lightning, or electrical surges. This protects sensitive electronics and extends the lifespan of the infrastructure.

8. User Guidance and Safety Signage:

- Clearly communicate safety guidelines through signage and user guidance. This includes information on safe charging practices, emergency protocols, and contact details for support.

Maintaining the integrity of the charging station infrastructure guarantees not only the reliability of the service but also prioritizes user safety. By addressing wear and tear, weather-related damages, and potential safety concerns, operators can uphold the quality and trustworthiness of their charging infrastructure.

Remote Monitoring: Proactive Oversight for Optimal Performance

Remote monitoring systems play a crucial role in the maintenance and management of electric vehicle (EV) charging stations, providing real-time insights and facilitating proactive measures:

1. Real-Time Data Collection:

- Remote monitoring systems continuously collect and transmit real-time data on the performance of charging stations. This includes information on energy consumption, charging sessions, and station health.

2. Fault Detection and Alerts:

- Automated monitoring enables the detection of faults or anomalies in charging station operation. Operators receive immediate alerts, allowing them to respond promptly and prevent potential issues from escalating.

3. Performance Metrics Analysis:

- Analyzing performance metrics, such as charging speed, efficiency, and user interactions, aids in identifying areas for improvement and optimizing the overall operation of the charging infrastructure.

4. Predictive Maintenance:

- By analyzing historical data and performance trends, remote monitoring systems can predict potential issues before they occur. This enables operators to schedule proactive maintenance, minimizing downtime and ensuring continuous service availability.

5. Energy Management:

- Monitoring energy consumption patterns assists in optimizing energy management. Operators can adjust charging parameters, implement load balancing, and contribute to grid stability based on real-time insights.

6. User Experience Enhancement:

- Monitoring user interactions and charging sessions helps operators understand user behavior and preferences. This data can be utilized to enhance the overall user experience, tailoring services to meet user expectations.

7. Cost-Efficient Operations:

- Proactive maintenance and issue resolution through remote monitoring contribute to cost-efficient operations. By addressing issues promptly, operators can avoid extensive repairs and reduce overall operational costs.

8. Remote Diagnostics:

- Remote monitoring allows for remote diagnostics of charging station components. Operators can assess the status of stations without physical presence, streamlining troubleshooting and maintenance efforts.

9. Data Security Measures:

- Implementing robust security measures in remote monitoring systems ensures the confidentiality and integrity of data. This is essential for protecting user information and maintaining the trust of stakeholders.

Incorporating remote monitoring systems into charging station management practices empowers operators to maintain optimal performance, enhance user experiences, and contribute to the overall efficiency and reliability of the charging infrastructure.

Section 7.2: User Support and Customer Service

Why is User Support and Customer Service Important?

User support and customer service are pivotal components of operating and managing charging stations, contributing to the success and sustainability of the electric vehicle (EV) charging business. Here's why they are crucial:

1. Enhanced User Experience:

- User support and customer service contribute to a positive and seamless experience for EV drivers. Prompt assistance and clear communication foster user satisfaction and trust in the charging infrastructure.

2. Issue Resolution and Technical Assistance:

- Offering reliable user support ensures that EV drivers receive assistance in case of issues, such as charging interruptions, payment concerns, or technical difficulties.

Technical assistance provided promptly helps minimize user inconvenience.

3. Building User Trust and Confidence:

- Effective customer service builds trust and confidence among EV users. Knowing that support is readily available in case of need encourages users to choose and rely on the charging infrastructure.

4. Educational Support:

- User support plays a role in educating EV drivers about optimal charging practices, station functionalities, and any specific requirements. This enhances user awareness and promotes safe and efficient use of the charging stations.

5. Accessibility for Diverse User Needs:

- Providing customer service accessible through various channels, such as helplines, emails, or online chat, ensures that users can seek assistance in their preferred way. This accommodates diverse user needs and preferences.

6. Feedback Collection and Improvement:

- Customer service serves as a valuable avenue for collecting user feedback. Understanding user experiences and addressing their suggestions helps in continuous improvement of the charging station services.

7. Resolving Payment and Billing Inquiries:

- Efficient customer service handles payment and billing inquiries promptly, ensuring transparent and accurate transactions. This contributes to user confidence in the financial aspects of using charging stations.

8. Emergency Response:

- In emergency situations or safety concerns, user support is crucial for guiding users on appropriate actions and coordinating with relevant authorities. This enhances overall user safety during charging sessions.

9. User Retention and Loyalty:

- Exceptional customer service contributes to user retention and loyalty. Satisfied users are more likely to choose the same charging infrastructure for their future EV needs and recommend it to others.

In essence, user support and customer service are integral components that not only address immediate user needs but also contribute to the long-term success, reputation, and sustainability of the EV charging business.

24/7 Customer Support: Always There When You Need Us

Ensuring round-the-clock customer support is a commitment to providing continuous assistance and a seamless experience for electric vehicle (EV) drivers. Here's why 24/7 customer support is a valuable component of charging station operations:

1. Immediate Issue Resolution:

- Offering 24/7 support ensures that EV drivers can receive immediate assistance in case of issues, such as charging interruptions, technical glitches, or payment concerns, regardless of the time of day or night.

2. Emergency Situations:

- In emergency situations or safety concerns, having 24/7 support is critical. Users can quickly access assistance and receive guidance on appropriate actions, contributing to overall user safety during charging sessions.

3. Global Accessibility:

- EV drivers may use charging stations at any time, including outside regular business hours. 24/7 customer support accommodates users in different time zones, providing a global solution for diverse charging needs.

4. Enhanced User Confidence:

- Knowing that customer support is available around the clock builds user confidence. This assurance encourages users to rely on the charging infrastructure, promoting trust and loyalty.

5. Flexibility for Users' Schedules:

- Electric vehicle drivers have varying schedules, and some may prefer to charge their vehicles during non-traditional hours. 24/7 customer support ensures that assistance is available whenever users choose to charge their EVs.

6. Real-Time Issue Monitoring:

- Continuous support enables real-time monitoring of charging stations. Operators can promptly address issues, monitor charging sessions, and ensure the optimal performance of the infrastructure.

7. User-Friendly Experience:

- A user-friendly experience is a key aspect of 24/7 support. Accessible through multiple channels, such as helplines, emails, or online chat, it provides users the flexibility to seek assistance in their preferred way.

8. Global Travel Support:

- For users traveling across different regions or countries, having 24/7 support ensures they can access assistance regardless of their location, contributing to a seamless charging experience.

In summary, 24/7 customer support reflects a commitment to user satisfaction, safety, and accessibility, making it an essential component of a well-rounded and reliable EV charging infrastructure.

User Education Programs: Empowering EV Drivers for a Sustainable Future

User education programs play a crucial role in ensuring that electric vehicle (EV) drivers are well-informed, confident, and adopt efficient charging practices. Here's why implementing user education programs is important and how they can be executed effectively:

Importance of User Education Programs:

1. Efficient Charging Practices:

   - Education programs guide users on optimal charging practices, including charging at off-peak hours, utilizing fast-charging appropriately, and avoiding unnecessary strain on the grid. This enhances the overall efficiency of the charging infrastructure.

2. Station Protocols Understanding:

   - Users gain insights into station protocols, such as proper cable handling, payment processes, and emergency procedures. This knowledge contributes to a smooth and safe charging experience.

3. Range Anxiety Alleviation:

   - Addressing common concerns like range anxiety, education programs provide information on the expanding charging network, helping users feel more confident about the availability of charging stations during their journeys.

4. Environmental Awareness:

   - Promoting the environmental benefits of EVs and sustainable charging practices fosters a sense of responsibility among users. Education programs can highlight the positive impact of EV adoption on reducing carbon emissions.

5. User Safety:

   - Users learn about safety measures during charging, including avoiding cable hazards, recognizing station indicators, and responding to emergency situations. This ensures a secure charging environment.

6. Charging Cost Understanding:

- Providing information on charging costs, different pricing models, and the factors influencing costs helps users make informed decisions about their charging habits and manage their expenses effectively.

7. Public and Workplace Charging Etiquette:

- Users are educated on charging etiquette, emphasizing considerations for shared public stations or workplace charging environments. This fosters a collaborative and respectful charging community.

Implementation Strategies:

1. Online Resources:

- Create online resources such as videos, tutorials, and FAQs on the charging infrastructure website. These resources should be easily accessible for users seeking information.

2. In-App Guidance:

- Integrate educational content within charging apps. Users can access relevant information directly through the app, enhancing their understanding of station features and practices.

3. Interactive Workshops and Webinars:

- Host interactive workshops or webinars where users can participate in Q&A sessions, receive live demonstrations, and engage with experts to enhance their knowledge.

4. Collaboration with EV Manufacturers:

- Collaborate with EV manufacturers to include educational materials in vehicle manuals or infotainment systems. This ensures that users receive information directly from the source.

5. Community Outreach Programs:

- Organize community outreach programs at charging stations, EV events, or local gatherings. Engage with users directly, answer their questions, and distribute educational materials.

6. Incentives for Participation:

- Provide incentives, such as discounts or promotional offers, for users who actively participate in educational programs. This encourages user engagement and enhances the effectiveness of the initiatives.

By prioritizing user education through various channels, operators can empower EV drivers with the knowledge they need for efficient, safe, and sustainable charging practices.

Mobile Apps and Platforms: Powering Seamless EV Charging Experiences

Why Mobile Apps and Platforms are Important:

1. Real-Time Information Access:

A Guide to the EV Charging Business

- Mobile apps provide EV drivers with real-time information about the availability of charging stations, current charging statuses, and anticipated wait times. This ensures users make informed decisions based on up-to-date data.

2. Convenient Session Management:

- Users can initiate, monitor, and manage charging sessions through mobile apps, offering a convenient and user-friendly interface. This includes functionalities like starting or stopping a charging session, viewing session history, and monitoring charging progress.

3. Support Ticket Systems:

- Implementing support ticket systems within mobile apps allows users to easily report issues, seek assistance, or provide feedback. This streamlined communication channel ensures prompt response and issue resolution.

4. Payment and Billing Integration:

- Mobile platforms facilitate seamless payment and billing integration, allowing users to make secure transactions within the app. This enhances the financial transparency of charging sessions.

5. User Account Management:

- Users can create and manage their accounts through mobile apps, enabling them to personalize preferences, track charging history, and access loyalty programs or membership benefits.

6. Navigation and Location Services:

- Integration with navigation and location services assists users in finding nearby charging stations. This feature is particularly valuable for users on the go, ensuring efficient route planning.

7. Notifications and Alerts:

- Mobile apps send notifications and alerts to users, informing them about charging session completion, station availability, or any important updates. This keeps users informed and engaged with the charging infrastructure.

8. User Authentication and Security:

- Mobile platforms ensure secure user authentication, protecting user accounts and personal information. Robust security measures build trust among users and contribute to the overall safety of the charging ecosystem.

9. Integration with Vehicle Telematics:

- Integrating with vehicle telematics allows the app to provide users with additional insights, such as battery status, range estimation, and suggested charging times. This enhances the overall user experience.

10. Promotion of Sustainable Practices:

- Mobile apps can include features that promote sustainable practices, such as providing information on renewable energy usage, carbon savings, and environmental impact. This aligns with the growing emphasis on green initiatives.

By leveraging mobile apps and platforms, operators can offer a comprehensive and user-centric solution, empowering EV drivers with the tools they need for efficient, convenient, and sustainable charging experiences.

Feedback Mechanisms: Fostering Continuous Improvement in EV Charging Services

Importance of Feedback Mechanisms:

1. User-Centric Service Enhancement:

- Feedback mechanisms place users at the center of service improvement. By actively seeking and analyzing user input, operators can tailor services to better meet the needs and expectations of the EV community.

2. Identifying Areas for Improvement:

- Regular feedback provides insights into specific areas that may require improvement, whether related to station reliability, user experience, payment processes, or additional amenities. This targeted information is invaluable for refining services.

3. Enhanced User Satisfaction:

- Addressing user concerns and making improvements based on feedback directly contributes to enhanced user satisfaction. Satisfied users are more likely to continue using the charging infrastructure and recommend it to others.

4. Quality Assurance:

- Establishing feedback mechanisms serves as a quality assurance measure. It helps operators ensure that charging stations consistently meet high standards, addressing any issues before they impact a broader user base.

5. Community Engagement:

- Encouraging user feedback fosters community engagement. Users feel more involved in the charging ecosystem, leading to a sense of ownership and shared responsibility for maintaining a reliable and efficient infrastructure.

6. Proactive Issue Resolution:

- Promptly addressing concerns raised through feedback mechanisms demonstrates a commitment to proactive issue resolution. This responsiveness builds trust and confidence among users.

7. Innovation and Adaptation:

- User input can spark innovative ideas and prompt the adoption of new technologies or features. Feedback mechanisms facilitate the identification of trends, allowing operators to adapt to evolving user expectations and industry advancements.

Implementation of Feedback Mechanisms:

1. Digital Surveys and Forms:

- Utilize digital surveys and feedback forms accessible through mobile apps, websites, or station interfaces. Ensure that these surveys cover various aspects of the user experience, from station functionality to payment processes.

2. In-App Feedback Channels:

- Incorporate feedback channels directly within mobile apps, providing users with a convenient platform to share their experiences, report issues, and suggest improvements.

3. User Community Forums:

- Establish online forums or communities where users can discuss their experiences, share insights, and provide feedback. This platform encourages collaborative problem-solving and idea generation.

4. Customer Support Interaction:

- Leverage customer support interactions as an avenue for gathering feedback. Encourage users to share their thoughts during support calls or through dedicated feedback tickets.

5. Social Media Engagement:

- Monitor social media platforms for user comments, reviews, and mentions. Engage with users in these spaces to gather feedback and address concerns publicly, showcasing a commitment to transparency.

6. Regular Surveys and Focus Groups:

- Conduct periodic surveys or organize focus groups to delve deeper into specific topics or areas for improvement. These structured approaches can provide detailed insights from a targeted audience.

7. Incentives for Feedback:

- Offer incentives, such as discounts or promotional benefits, for users who actively participate in providing feedback. This encourages a higher level of engagement and input.

By actively seeking and valuing user feedback, operators can create a dynamic and user-centric charging infrastructure that evolves to meet the changing needs and expectations of the electric vehicle community.

Section 7.3: Data Management and Analytics

Why Data Management and Analytics are Crucial for EV Charging Stations:

1. Optimizing Charging Infrastructure:

- Data analytics provide insights into charging station usage patterns, enabling operators to optimize the placement, capacity, and functionality of charging stations for maximum efficiency.

2. User Behavior Analysis:

- By analyzing user behavior, such as peak charging times and session durations, operators can tailor services to meet specific user needs, enhancing the overall charging experience.

3. Predictive Maintenance:

- Utilizing data analytics allows operators to predict potential equipment failures or maintenance needs, enabling proactive measures to minimize downtime and ensure the reliability of charging stations.

4. Energy Consumption Optimization:

- Data management helps operators optimize energy consumption by understanding the energy demand at different times. This information contributes to more efficient energy distribution and usage.

5. Financial Planning and Billing Accuracy:

- Accurate data management supports precise financial planning by providing insights into revenue generation, user preferences, and charging costs. This, in turn, ensures accurate billing and financial stability.

6. Grid Integration and Load Management:

- Integrating data analytics with the electrical grid enables operators to manage the load efficiently. This is particularly important in preventing grid overload during peak usage times and contributing to grid stability.

7. Customized User Experiences:

- Data-driven insights enable operators to create customized user experiences, from personalized recommendations to targeted promotions. This enhances user engagement and satisfaction.

8. Environmental Impact Assessment:

- Operators can assess the environmental impact of charging stations by analyzing data on energy sources, carbon emissions saved, and overall sustainability. This information contributes to eco-friendly practices.

Implementation of Data Management and Analytics:

1. Real-Time Monitoring Systems:

- Implement real-time monitoring systems that capture data on charging sessions, equipment status, and user interactions. This data forms the foundation for analytics and decision-making.

2. Advanced Metering Infrastructure (AMI):

- Deploy advanced metering infrastructure to collect detailed information on energy consumption, charging rates, and user behavior. This data is valuable for optimizing charging station performance.

3. Cloud-Based Data Storage:

- Utilize cloud-based storage solutions to securely store and manage large volumes of data. Cloud infrastructure facilitates accessibility, scalability, and collaboration in data analytics.

4. Machine Learning Algorithms:

- Employ machine learning algorithms to analyze complex patterns in charging behavior, predict usage trends, and enhance predictive maintenance capabilities for charging infrastructure.

5. Integration with Smart Grids:

- Integrate charging stations with smart grids to exchange data on energy demand, grid status, and load balancing. This integration enhances grid management and contributes to overall energy efficiency.

6. User Analytics for Personalization:

- Analyze user data to understand preferences, charging habits, and user journeys. This information enables operators to personalize services, recommend charging times, and offer targeted promotions.

7. Security and Compliance Measures:

- Implement robust security measures to protect user data and ensure compliance with data protection regulations. Building trust through secure data management is crucial for user confidence.

8. Periodic Data Audits:

- Conduct periodic data audits to ensure the accuracy and reliability of the collected information. Regular audits contribute to maintaining the integrity of the data management system.

By harnessing the power of data management and analytics, operators can not only improve the operational efficiency of charging stations but also enhance the overall user experience, contribute to grid stability, and promote sustainable charging practices.

Charging Session Data: Enhancing Charging Infrastructure Efficiency

Importance of Charging Session Data:

1. Usage Pattern Analysis:

   - Analyzing data from charging sessions provides valuable insights into usage patterns, helping operators understand when and how frequently stations are utilized. This information aids in optimizing station placement and capacity.

2. Peak Hour Identification:

   - By examining charging session data, operators can identify peak hours and demand trends. This knowledge allows for proactive measures, such as additional staffing during busy periods or implementing dynamic pricing to manage peak demand.

3. User Behavior Understanding:

   - Charging session data offers a deep understanding of user behaviors, including preferred charging times, session durations, and user interactions with station interfaces. This insight enables operators to tailor services to user needs.

4. Operational Efficiency Enhancement:

- Utilizing data from charging sessions supports operational efficiency improvements. Operators can streamline maintenance schedules, allocate resources effectively, and ensure that charging stations are available when users need them.

5. Optimizing Charging Station Placement:

- Detailed data on charging session locations aids in optimizing station placement. Operators can identify high-traffic areas and strategically position new stations to meet growing demand.

Implementation of Charging Session Data Analysis:

1. Real-Time Monitoring Systems:

- Implement real-time monitoring systems that capture and store data from each charging session. These systems should provide comprehensive information, including start and end times, energy consumption, and user identification.

2. Usage Reports and Dashboards:

- Generate regular reports and dashboards summarizing charging session data. These visual representations allow operators to quickly grasp usage patterns, peak hours, and other relevant metrics.

3. User Surveys and Feedback Integration:

- Integrate user surveys and feedback mechanisms into charging station interfaces or mobile apps. Combine user input with charging session data to gain a holistic understanding of user preferences and satisfaction levels.

4. Predictive Analytics for Maintenance:

- Apply predictive analytics to charging session data for proactive maintenance planning. Identify potential issues before they escalate, ensuring optimal station performance and minimizing downtime.

5. Dynamic Pricing Strategies:

- Leverage charging session data to implement dynamic pricing strategies during peak hours. Adjust pricing based on demand, encouraging users to charge during off-peak times for cost savings.

6. User Behavior Analytics:

- Use user behavior analytics to understand charging habits, such as preferred charging durations and common charging locations. This information informs decisions on station capacity, charging speed, and user interface improvements.

7. Machine Learning Algorithms:

- Implement machine learning algorithms to uncover hidden patterns and trends within charging session data. These algorithms can provide nuanced insights that contribute to more informed decision-making.

8. Data Privacy and Security Measures:

- Prioritize data privacy and security when handling charging session data. Implement robust measures to protect user information, ensuring compliance with relevant data protection regulations.

By systematically collecting and analyzing charging session data, operators can fine-tune their charging infrastructure, improve user experiences, and proactively address operational challenges, ultimately contributing to the overall success of the EV charging business.

Predictive Analytics for Proactive Charging Infrastructure Management

Importance of Predictive Analytics:

1. Anticipating Charging Demands:

- Predictive analytics analyze historical charging data to forecast future demands. By understanding patterns and trends, operators can anticipate when and where charging stations will experience increased usage.

2. Proactive Resource Allocation:

- Armed with predictions from analytics, operators can proactively allocate resources. This includes ensuring sufficient staffing during peak hours, maintaining optimal charging station functionality, and addressing potential issues before they impact users.

3. Optimizing Station Availability:

- Predictive analytics help optimize station availability by adjusting resources based on expected demand. This ensures that charging stations are adequately prepared to meet user needs, minimizing wait times and enhancing overall user satisfaction.

4. Dynamic Pricing Strategies:

- Utilizing predictive analytics allows operators to implement dynamic pricing strategies. By forecasting peak demand periods, operators can adjust pricing dynamically, encouraging users to charge during off-peak times for cost savings.

5. Efficient Maintenance Planning:

- Predictive analytics contribute to efficient maintenance planning. By identifying potential equipment failures or maintenance needs in advance, operators can schedule maintenance during periods of lower demand, minimizing disruptions to users.

Implementation of Predictive Analytics:

1. Historical Charging Data Analysis:

- Begin by analyzing historical charging data to identify patterns and trends. This forms the basis for predictive models that anticipate future charging demands.

2. Machine Learning Algorithms:

- Employ machine learning algorithms to build predictive models. These algorithms can recognize complex patterns in charging behavior, considering factors such as time of day, day of the week, and seasonal variations.

3. Real-Time Monitoring Integration:

- Integrate real-time monitoring systems with predictive analytics. This ensures that predictions are continuously updated based on the latest charging session data, allowing for immediate adjustments to resource allocation.

4. Dynamic Resource Allocation:

- Develop strategies for dynamic resource allocation based on predictive analytics. This may involve adjusting staffing levels, optimizing station capacity, or implementing dynamic pricing during forecasted peak hours.

5. User Feedback Integration:

- Incorporate user feedback into predictive models. User insights provide valuable context to the data, enhancing the accuracy of predictions and ensuring that user preferences are considered in proactive adjustments.

6. Continuous Model Refinement:

- Continuously refine predictive models based on ongoing data analysis. As charging behaviors evolve or new trends emerge, the predictive analytics should adapt to reflect the changing dynamics of the charging ecosystem.

7. User Communication Strategies:

- Develop communication strategies to inform users about expected demand patterns and potential peak times. This proactive approach helps manage user expectations and encourages strategic charging behavior.

8. Privacy and Ethical Considerations:

- Prioritize privacy and ethical considerations when implementing predictive analytics. Ensure that user data is handled responsibly and in compliance with relevant regulations, maintaining trust in the charging infrastructure.

By embracing predictive analytics, operators can transform reactive management into proactive strategies, providing a more seamless and efficient charging experience for users while optimizing the overall performance of the charging infrastructure.

Energy Consumption Analysis: Enhancing Charging Station Efficiency

Importance of Energy Consumption Analysis:

1. Optimizing Station Efficiency:

- Energy consumption analysis allows operators to identify inefficiencies in charging stations, enabling optimization of energy usage. This optimization contributes to the overall efficiency and reliability of the charging infrastructure.

2. Identifying Energy-Saving Initiatives:

- By closely monitoring energy consumption patterns, operators can identify opportunities for energy-saving initiatives. This may involve adjusting charging station settings, implementing energy-efficient technologies, or exploring renewable energy sources.

3. Cost-Efficient Operations:

- Understanding energy consumption helps in managing operational costs. By identifying ways to minimize energy waste, operators can ensure that the charging stations operate in a cost-efficient manner, contributing to the financial sustainability of the business.

4. Sustainable Operations:

- Energy consumption analysis is integral to sustainable operations. By adopting eco-friendly practices and reducing energy waste, operators can contribute to environmental sustainability, aligning the charging business with broader ecological goals.

Implementation of Energy Consumption Analysis:

1. Real-Time Energy Monitoring Systems:

- Implement real-time energy monitoring systems within charging stations. These systems should capture data on energy consumption during each charging session, providing insights into usage patterns and station efficiency.

2. Energy Consumption Reports:

- Generate regular reports summarizing energy consumption data. These reports should highlight trends, peak usage times, and areas where energy-saving initiatives can be implemented. Visual representations aid in understanding consumption patterns.

3. Energy Efficiency Technologies:

- Explore and implement energy-efficient technologies within charging stations. This may include advanced power management systems, smart charging algorithms, and the use of energy-efficient components to reduce overall consumption.

4. Renewable Energy Integration:

- Consider integrating renewable energy sources into the charging station infrastructure. This can include solar panels, wind turbines, or other clean energy solutions to offset electricity consumption and promote sustainability.

5. User Education on Energy Conservation:

- Educate users on energy conservation practices. Provide information on the environmental impact of charging choices, and encourage users to adopt energy-efficient habits, such as charging during off-peak hours.

6. Dynamic Power Management:

- Implement dynamic power management strategies based on energy consumption analysis. This involves adjusting charging rates or station availability during peak energy demand times to optimize resource usage.

7. Collaboration with Energy Providers:

- Collaborate with energy providers to explore opportunities for energy efficiency programs. This collaboration may involve negotiating favorable energy rates, participating in demand response initiatives, or accessing energy-saving incentives.

8. Continuous Improvement Initiatives:

- Foster a culture of continuous improvement by regularly reviewing and updating energy consumption analysis strategies. As technology evolves and new energy-saving solutions emerge, operators should adapt to stay at the forefront of efficiency.

By conducting thorough energy consumption analysis, charging station operators can not only optimize operational efficiency but also contribute to cost savings, environmental sustainability, and a positive user experience.

User Behavior Insights: Tailoring Charging Services Through Data Analysis

Importance of User Behavior Insights:

1. Service Customization:

- Extracting insights from user behavior data allows operators to customize charging services. By understanding user preferences and habits, operators can tailor offerings to meet the diverse needs of their user base.

2. Enhanced User Experiences:

- Utilizing user behavior insights enhances overall user experiences. This involves optimizing charging station interfaces, streamlining user interactions, and implementing features that align with the way users prefer to charge their electric vehicles.

3. Demand-Driven Adjustments:

- By analyzing user behavior, operators can make demand-driven adjustments. This may involve modifying station availability, adjusting charging rates during peak times, or expanding services based on identified user demands.

4. Market Demand Alignment:

- Understanding user behavior aligns charging services with evolving market demands. As user preferences and expectations change, operators can adapt their offerings to remain competitive and meet the evolving needs of electric vehicle owners.

Implementation of User Behavior Insights:

1. User Behavior Analytics Platforms:

- Implement user behavior analytics platforms that capture and analyze data from charging station interactions. These platforms should provide detailed insights into user preferences, charging habits, and common user pain points.

2. Charging Session Surveys:

- Incorporate surveys within charging station interfaces or mobile apps to gather direct feedback from users. This qualitative data complements quantitative analytics, providing a more comprehensive understanding of user experiences.

3. User Persona Development:

- Develop user personas based on behavior insights. Categorize users into different personas to better understand their preferences, charging habits, and expectations. This helps in tailoring services to specific user segments.

4. Interface Optimization:

- Optimize charging station interfaces based on user behavior insights. Ensure that the user interface is intuitive, user-friendly, and aligns with how users prefer to interact with the charging station.

5. Personalized Charging Recommendations:

- Provide personalized charging recommendations based on user behavior. This may involve suggesting optimal charging times, notifying users of nearby stations, or offering promotions aligned with individual charging patterns.

6. Communication Strategies:

- Develop communication strategies based on user behavior. Tailor marketing messages, notifications, and educational content to resonate with the preferences and habits of the target audience.

7. User Engagement Programs:

- Create user engagement programs that incentivize desired behaviors. This could include loyalty programs, rewards for off-peak charging, or promotions that align with identified user preferences.

8. Continuous Iteration:

- Adopt a continuous iteration approach based on user behavior insights. Regularly review and update services, interfaces, and offerings to reflect changing user dynamics and preferences.

9. Privacy and Transparency:

- Prioritize user privacy and transparency when utilizing behavior insights. Clearly communicate data usage practices and ensure compliance with privacy regulations to maintain user trust.

By leveraging user behavior insights, charging station operators can cultivate a deeper understanding of their users, leading to more tailored services, enhanced user experiences, and a heightened ability to adapt to the ever-changing landscape of the electric vehicle market.

Security Measures for Safeguarding User Data in Charging Stations

Importance of Security Measures:

1. User Trust and Confidence:

- Robust security measures instill user trust and confidence. Users need assurance that their personal and transactional data is handled securely, fostering a positive perception of the charging station's reliability.

2. Privacy Compliance:

- Implementing security measures ensures compliance with privacy regulations. Adhering to data protection laws is crucial for maintaining the legal integrity of the charging station operation and protecting user rights.

3. Prevention of Unauthorized Access:

- Security measures are essential for preventing unauthorized access to sensitive user information. Unauthorized access can lead to data breaches, compromising user privacy and potentially damaging the reputation of the charging station.

4. Data Integrity and Confidentiality:

- Ensuring data integrity and confidentiality is paramount. Users expect that their information remains private and is not tampered with, emphasizing the importance of secure data storage and transmission.

Implementation of Security Measures:

1. End-to-End Encryption:

- Implement end-to-end encryption for data transmitted between charging stations and backend systems. This encryption method ensures that data remains confidential and secure during transit.

2. Secure Authentication Protocols:

- Utilize secure authentication protocols for user access to charging station interfaces and mobile apps. This prevents unauthorized individuals from gaining access to user accounts and transaction details.

3. Secure Data Storage Practices:

- Follow secure data storage practices to safeguard user information. Utilize encryption for stored data, implement access controls, and regularly audit data storage systems for vulnerabilities.

4. Regular Security Audits:

- Conduct regular security audits to identify and address potential vulnerabilities. This includes penetration testing, code reviews, and assessments of the overall cybersecurity posture of the charging station infrastructure.

5. Incident Response Plan:

- Develop and maintain an incident response plan to handle security breaches or data incidents effectively. A well-defined plan ensures a prompt and coordinated response to mitigate the impact of any security incidents.

6. User Education on Security Practices:

- Educate users on security best practices. Provide guidance on creating secure passwords, using secure Wi-Fi networks, and recognizing potential phishing attempts to enhance overall cybersecurity awareness.

7. Multi-Factor Authentication:

- Implement multi-factor authentication to add an extra layer of security to user accounts. This ensures that even if credentials are compromised, additional verification steps are required for access.

8. Regular Software Updates:

- Keep all software components up to date with the latest security patches. Regularly update charging station firmware, backend systems, and any third-party software to address known vulnerabilities.

9. Privacy Policy Transparency:

- Maintain transparency through a clear and concise privacy policy. Communicate how user data is collected, processed, and protected, reinforcing trust through openness about data handling practices.

10. Employee Training:

- Provide comprehensive training for charging station employees on cybersecurity practices. Employees play a crucial role in maintaining data security, and ongoing training ensures awareness of the latest threats and preventive measures.

11. Collaboration with Cybersecurity Experts:

- Collaborate with cybersecurity experts or consult with security firms to assess and enhance the overall security posture. Expert input can provide valuable insights and recommendations for improving security measures.

By diligently implementing and continuously updating security measures, charging stations can create a secure environment for users, protect sensitive data, and demonstrate a commitment to maintaining the highest standards of privacy and cybersecurity.

Integration with Utility Systems: Enhancing Energy Efficiency and Grid Stability

Importance of Integration with Utility Systems:

1. Optimized Energy Distribution:

- Integration with utility systems allows charging stations to optimize energy distribution. By synchronizing with utility grids, stations can manage energy flow efficiently, preventing overloads and ensuring balanced distribution.

2. Facilitating Demand Response:

- Integration enables charging stations to participate in demand response programs. By responding to signals from utility providers during peak demand periods, stations can contribute to grid stability and support overall energy management efforts.

3. Grid Stability and Reliability:

- Contributing to grid stability is crucial for the reliability of the overall energy infrastructure. Charging stations, when integrated with utility systems, can play a role in stabilizing the grid by adapting charging patterns based on grid conditions.

4. Load Balancing:

- Integration supports load balancing across the utility grid. Charging stations can coordinate with the grid to distribute the load evenly, preventing localized strain on specific grid segments and enhancing the overall efficiency of energy distribution.

Implementation of Integration with Utility Systems:

1. Smart Grid Connectivity:

- Implement smart grid connectivity to enable real-time communication between charging stations and the utility grid. This connectivity allows stations to receive grid status updates and adjust charging operations accordingly.

2. Demand Forecasting and Management:

- Utilize demand forecasting tools to anticipate peak usage periods. Charging stations can adjust their operations based on forecasts, contributing to demand management strategies that align with grid conditions.

3. Dynamic Pricing Integration:

- Integrate with dynamic pricing models from utility providers. Charging stations can adapt charging rates based on real-time pricing signals, encouraging users to charge during periods of lower electricity costs.

4. Grid-Friendly Charging Algorithms:

   - Develop and implement grid-friendly charging algorithms. These algorithms consider grid conditions, such as load levels and stability, to adjust the charging speed and timing, ensuring a harmonious interaction with the utility grid.

5. Bi-Directional Charging:

   - Explore bi-directional charging capabilities. This allows charging stations not only to draw energy from the grid but also to feed excess energy back into the grid during specific conditions, enhancing grid stability and supporting renewable energy integration.

6. Collaboration with Utility Providers:

   - Foster collaboration with utility providers. Establish communication channels to exchange data, align strategies, and ensure seamless integration between charging stations and utility systems.

7. Grid Monitoring and Reporting:

   - Implement grid monitoring and reporting features. Charging stations can provide data on their energy consumption, grid interactions, and contributions to demand response programs, facilitating transparency and accountability.

8. Regulatory Compliance:

   - Stay abreast of regulatory requirements related to grid integration. Ensure that charging stations comply with local regulations and standards governing interactions with utility systems.

9. Remote Control and Management:

- Enable remote control and management capabilities. This allows operators to adjust charging parameters, respond to grid events, and implement changes in real-time to align with utility system requirements.

10. Energy Storage Integration:

- Consider integrating energy storage solutions with charging stations. This enables storing excess energy during periods of low demand and releasing it during peak demand, further supporting grid stability.

Integration with utility systems empowers charging stations to become dynamic participants in the broader energy ecosystem. By aligning charging operations with grid conditions and contributing to demand response initiatives, integrated stations play a pivotal role in promoting energy efficiency, reliability, and sustainability.

CHAPTER 08

MARKETING AND PROMOTION

Marketing and Promotion: Navigating the EV Charging Landscape

Introduction:

The realm of marketing and promotion in the electric vehicle (EV) charging business is multifaceted, requiring a strategic approach to attract users, build brand recognition, and foster partnerships. This chapter delves into the intricacies of promoting your charging stations, addressing the diverse needs of EV users, and establishing a compelling brand presence.

Section 8.1: Attracting EV Users

1. Understanding the EV Community:

- Develop insights into the preferences and behaviors of the EV community. Tailor marketing strategies to resonate with the values and interests of electric vehicle users.

2. Targeted Online Campaigns:

- Leverage digital platforms for targeted online campaigns. Utilize social media, EV forums, and specialized websites to reach and engage with the EV user community.

3. Educational Content:

- Create educational content highlighting the benefits of your charging stations. Provide information on charging speeds, compatibility with different EV models, and the environmental impact of choosing electric transportation.

4. Loyalty Programs:

- Introduce loyalty programs to reward frequent users. Offer discounts, exclusive perks, or partnerships with local businesses to enhance the overall charging experience and encourage user loyalty.

Section 8.2: Branding and Marketing Strategies

1. Distinctive Branding:

- Establish a distinctive brand identity for your charging stations. Develop a logo, color scheme, and tagline that reflects the reliability, efficiency, and eco-friendly nature of your charging services.

2. User-Centric Messaging:

- Craft user-centric messaging that emphasizes convenience, affordability, and sustainability. Communicate how your charging stations cater to the needs and preferences of EV users.

3. Seamless User Experience:

- Ensure a seamless and user-friendly experience at your charging stations. Emphasize simplicity in your marketing messages, highlighting features like easy payment options, user interfaces, and accessibility.

4. Collaborative Marketing with Automakers:

- Collaborate with automakers for joint marketing initiatives. Aligning with vehicle manufacturers can enhance your station's visibility and credibility within the EV community.

Section 8.3: Partnerships and Collaborations

1. Collaborations with Local Businesses:

- Form partnerships with local businesses to cross-promote services. Consider collaborations with nearby cafes, shopping centers, or recreational spots to create synergies that benefit both parties.

2. Integration with Navigation Apps:

- Ensure your charging stations are integrated into popular navigation apps. Users often rely on navigation tools to find charging stations, so visibility in these apps is crucial for attracting users.

3. Corporate Partnerships for Workplace Charging:

- Establish partnerships with corporations to provide workplace charging solutions. Workplace charging programs contribute to employee satisfaction and align with corporate sustainability goals.

4. Sponsorship of EV Events:

- Sponsor or participate in EV-related events, conferences, and exhibitions. These platforms offer opportunities to showcase your charging stations, connect with potential users, and stay abreast of industry trends.

5. Loyalty Programs with EV Manufacturers:

- Collaborate with EV manufacturers to offer joint loyalty programs. This can involve exclusive benefits for users of specific EV models, fostering brand loyalty and expanding your user base.

6. Community Engagement Programs:

- Implement community engagement programs. Sponsor local events, support environmental initiatives, and actively participate in community activities to build a positive and socially responsible brand image.

7. Cross-Promotions with Sustainable Brands:

- Collaborate with other sustainable brands for cross-promotions. This can involve joint marketing campaigns, shared promotional materials, or co-branded initiatives that resonate with environmentally conscious consumers.

8. Public Relations Efforts:

- Invest in public relations efforts to garner positive media coverage. Highlight your charging stations' contributions to sustainability and showcase success stories and positive user experiences.

Effective marketing and strategic partnerships play a crucial role in attracting and retaining EV users. By aligning with the values of the EV community, creating a strong brand identity, and forming meaningful collaborations, your charging business can establish a prominent presence in the electric mobility landscape.

Section 8.1: Attracting EV Users

1. Understanding the EV Community:

- Develop insights into the preferences and behaviors of the EV community. Tailor marketing strategies to resonate with the values and interests of electric vehicle users.

2. Targeted Online Campaigns:

- Leverage digital platforms for targeted online campaigns. Utilize social media, EV forums, and specialized websites to reach and engage with the EV user community.

3. Educational Content:

- Create educational content highlighting the benefits of your charging stations. Provide information on charging speeds, compatibility with different EV models, and the environmental impact of choosing electric transportation.

4. Loyalty Programs:

- Introduce loyalty programs to reward frequent users. Offer discounts, exclusive perks, or partnerships with local businesses to enhance the overall charging experience and encourage user loyalty.

Understanding the EV community is pivotal for any business operating in the electric vehicle (EV) charging industry. The EV community is diverse, consisting of individuals with varying interests, values, and motivations for choosing electric transportation. To effectively tailor marketing strategies, it is essential to delve into the following aspects of the EV community:

1. Environmental Consciousness:

- Understanding Green Values: Many individuals within the EV community are environmentally conscious and are motivated by a desire to reduce their carbon footprint. Tailoring marketing messages that emphasize the positive environmental impact of EV adoption can strongly resonate with this segment.

2. Technology Enthusiasts:

- Embracing Technological Advancements: A significant portion of the EV community comprises technology enthusiasts who appreciate innovation. Highlighting the cutting-edge technology in EVs, such as advanced battery systems and smart charging features, can capture the attention of this demographic.

3. Economic Considerations:

- Cost-Saving Drivers: Some individuals in the EV community are motivated by economic factors, including lower operating costs and potential long-term savings. Marketing strategies that emphasize the economic benefits of EV ownership, such as reduced fuel expenses and maintenance costs, can attract this segment.

4. Community Engagement:

- Building a Sense of Community: The EV community often values a sense of belonging and community. Marketing efforts can focus on creating forums, events, or online spaces where EV enthusiasts can connect, share experiences, and feel part of a larger movement.

5. Educational Needs:

- Providing Information: Many individuals considering or already part of the EV community may have informational needs. Creating content that educates about EV charging, technological advancements, and sustainability can be valuable for both current EV owners and those exploring the possibility of EV adoption.

6. Infrastructure Reliance:

- Dependence on Charging Infrastructure: As the EV community heavily relies on charging infrastructure, marketing efforts can highlight the accessibility and convenience of charging stations. Emphasizing the strategic placement of charging stations in key locations can be particularly appealing.

Understanding these facets enables businesses to craft marketing strategies that align with the values and interests of the EV community. Whether emphasizing the environmental benefits, technological advancements, economic advantages, or the sense of community, tailored approaches can foster stronger connections and resonate more effectively with potential and existing EV users.

To target online campaigns effectively for the EV community, follow these steps:

1. Identify Key Platforms:

- Determine the most frequented online platforms within the EV community. This may include social media channels (e.g., Facebook, Twitter, LinkedIn), EV forums, and specialized websites dedicated to electric vehicles.

2. Create Engaging Content:

- Develop content that aligns with the interests of the EV community. Highlight the environmental benefits of EVs, share charging tips, and showcase success stories to engage users.

3. Utilize Social Media:

- Establish a presence on popular social media platforms. Share relevant content regularly, participate in discussions, and leverage targeted advertising options to reach specific demographics interested in EVs.

4. Engage in EV Forums:

- Join and actively participate in EV forums and online communities. Engage in discussions, address user queries, and subtly promote your charging stations where appropriate.

5. Collaborate with Influencers:

- Identify and collaborate with influencers in the EV space. Their endorsement and promotion can significantly enhance the visibility of your charging stations among their followers.

6. Optimize for Search Engines:

- Ensure your online content is optimized for search engines (SEO). This helps your charging stations appear prominently in search results when users are looking for EV-related information.

7. Run Targeted Ads:

- Run targeted online advertisements focusing on EV-related keywords and interests. Platforms like Facebook and Google Ads allow you to reach specific demographics, ensuring your ads are seen by those interested in electric vehicles.

8. Utilize Email Marketing:

- Implement email marketing campaigns to keep the EV community informed about updates, promotions, and new features of your charging stations. Personalize messages to enhance user engagement.

9. Monitor Analytics:

- Regularly analyze the performance of your online campaigns using analytics tools. Track user engagement, click-through rates, and conversions to refine your strategies based on data-driven insights.

By strategically leveraging online platforms and tailoring content to the preferences of the EV community, you can effectively reach and engage with potential users of your charging stations.

Importance of Educational Content in EV Charging Business:

1. Informing Users:

- Educational content serves as a valuable resource to inform users about the specifics of your charging stations. Details on charging speeds and compatibility with different EV models help users make informed decisions.

2. Addressing User Concerns:

- Users may have concerns or questions about the charging process. Educational content addresses these concerns, offering clarity on how to use the stations, what to expect in terms of charging times, and compatibility with their specific EV model.

3. Promoting Environmental Benefits:

   - Highlighting the environmental impact of electric transportation creates awareness and aligns with the values of environmentally conscious users. Emphasize reduced carbon footprint and the positive contribution to sustainability.

4. Building Trust and Confidence:

   - Comprehensive and clear information builds trust. When users have a thorough understanding of how your charging stations work and their benefits, they are more likely to trust and choose your services.

5. Encouraging Adoption:

   - Users who understand the advantages of electric transportation and the convenience of your charging stations are more likely to adopt EVs. Educational content contributes to the broader goal of promoting the adoption of electric vehicles.

6. Differentiation from Competitors:

   - Providing detailed educational content sets your charging business apart from competitors. It demonstrates a commitment to transparency and user education, which can be a competitive advantage in the market.

7. Supporting User Experience:

- Educated users are more likely to have a positive experience with your charging stations. They know what to expect, reducing potential frustrations or uncertainties during the charging process.

8. Community Engagement:

- Educational content fosters community engagement. Sharing insights about EV technology, charging advancements, and environmental benefits creates a sense of community among your users.

9. SEO and Online Visibility:

- Educational content contributes to better search engine optimization (SEO). When users search for information related to EV charging, your content is more likely to appear in search results, increasing your online visibility.

In summary, educational content is pivotal for providing information, building trust, encouraging environmentally conscious choices, and ultimately driving the adoption of electric vehicles and the use of your charging stations. It plays a crucial role in creating an informed and engaged user base.

Loyalty Programs in EV Charging Business:

1. Rewarding Frequent Users:

- Loyalty programs aim to recognize and reward users who frequently utilize your charging stations. This recognition can be in the form of points, discounts, or other incentives.

2. Discounts on Charging Sessions:

- Offer loyalty program members discounted rates on their charging sessions. This provides an immediate benefit for their loyalty and encourages them to continue using your charging infrastructure.

3. Exclusive Perks:

- Provide exclusive perks to loyalty program members. This could include access to premium charging stations, priority service, or special events. Exclusive perks enhance the overall user experience.

4. Partnerships with Local Businesses:

- Collaborate with local businesses to extend benefits to loyalty program members. For example, partnerships with nearby cafes or shops could offer users discounts or special deals when they show proof of loyalty program membership.

5. Point Accumulation System:

- Implement a point-based system where users earn points for each charging session. Accumulated points can then be redeemed for discounts, free charging sessions, or other rewards.

6. Tiered Loyalty Levels:

- Create tiered loyalty levels based on usage frequency. As users move up in loyalty levels, they unlock additional benefits and rewards. This tiered approach encourages continued loyalty.

7. Personalized Offers:

- Tailor offers and rewards based on individual user behavior. Personalized incentives make the loyalty program more appealing and relevant to each user.

8. Promotional Events:

- Host promotional events exclusively for loyalty program members. This could include special charging events, product launches, or educational sessions.

9. Easy Enrollment and Tracking:

- Ensure that enrolling in the loyalty program is straightforward. Implement a user-friendly tracking system so members can easily monitor their loyalty points and redeem rewards.

10. Communication and Updates:

- Keep loyalty program members informed about new offers, upcoming events, and any changes to the program. Regular communication maintains engagement and encourages ongoing participation.

Implementing a well-designed loyalty program not only incentivizes users to choose your charging stations repeatedly but also fosters a sense of community and appreciation among your user base.

Section 8.2: Branding and Marketing Strategies

1. Distinctive Brand Identity:

- Develop a distinctive brand identity for your EV charging business. This includes a memorable logo, color scheme, and tagline that reflects the values of sustainability, innovation, and accessibility.

2. Targeted Messaging:

- Tailor your messaging to resonate with your target audience. Emphasize the environmental benefits of EV charging, the convenience of your stations, and the positive impact users can make by choosing electric transportation.

3. Online Presence:

- Establish a strong online presence through a user-friendly website and active participation in social media. Regularly update content, share user testimonials, and showcase the unique features of your charging stations.

4. Content Marketing:

- Create informative and engaging content related to electric vehicles, charging tips, and industry trends. Content marketing not only educates users but also positions your brand as an authority in the EV charging space.

5. Partnerships and Collaborations:

- Forge partnerships with EV manufacturers, local businesses, and environmental organizations. Collaborative efforts enhance your brand's credibility and extend your reach to new audiences.

6. User Testimonials and Case Studies:

- Highlight positive user experiences through testimonials and case studies. Real-life stories and successes create authenticity and build trust in your brand.

7. Community Engagement:

- Actively engage with the EV community through forums, social media groups, and local events. Participate in discussions, address user concerns, and demonstrate your commitment to community involvement.

8. Event Sponsorship:

- Sponsor or participate in events related to electric vehicles, sustainability, and technology. This not only increases brand visibility but also positions your business as a supporter of the larger EV ecosystem.

9. Innovative Advertising:

- Explore innovative advertising methods such as augmented reality, virtual reality, or interactive campaigns to capture the attention of tech-savvy and environmentally conscious audiences.

10. Consistent Branding Across Channels:

- Maintain consistency in branding across all channels. Whether it's your website, social media, or physical signage at charging stations, a cohesive brand image reinforces recognition and trust.

11. Green Certification and Awards:

- Pursue green certifications and awards that validate your commitment to sustainability. Displaying these accolades in your marketing materials reinforces your environmentally friendly brand positioning.

12. Customer Engagement Programs:

- Implement customer engagement programs, such as referral rewards or user-generated content campaigns. Encourage users to share their experiences and become advocates for your brand.

Effective branding and marketing strategies not only attract users to your charging stations but also create a positive perception of your business within the EV community and beyond.

Distinctive Branding in EV Charging Business:

Importance:

1. Recognition:

- Distinctive branding helps users easily identify and recognize your charging stations among others. A memorable logo and color scheme contribute to instant visual recognition.

2. Trust and Credibility:

- A well-crafted brand identity builds trust and credibility. Users are more likely to choose a charging station with a professional and distinctive brand, associating it with reliability and quality service.

3. Differentiation:

- In a competitive market, distinctive branding sets your charging stations apart. It differentiates your business from others, emphasizing your unique features and commitment to sustainability.

4. User Experience:

- A cohesive brand identity contributes to a positive user experience. Consistent branding across stations, websites, and promotional materials creates a seamless and professional impression.

5. Memorability:

- A distinctive logo and tagline make your brand memorable. Users who have a positive experience with your charging stations are more likely to remember and choose your services in the future.

6. Brand Recall:

- Distinctive branding enhances brand recall. When users see your logo or branding elements, it triggers memories of positive experiences, encouraging repeat business.

7. Marketing Effectiveness:

- Marketing efforts are more effective when supported by a distinctive brand. Clear and recognizable branding elements make promotional materials, online campaigns, and advertisements more impactful.

8. Alignment with Values:

- Your brand identity should align with the values of sustainability and eco-friendliness associated with electric vehicles. This alignment reinforces your commitment to environmental responsibility.

9. Professionalism:

- A well-designed and distinctive brand communicates professionalism. It conveys that your charging stations are part of a reliable and well-established network, instilling confidence in users.

10. Adaptability:

- As your charging business grows, a distinctive brand remains adaptable. It can evolve to encompass new services, locations, or partnerships while maintaining a recognizable core identity.

In summary, distinctive branding is crucial for building trust, standing out in a crowded market, and creating a positive and memorable experience for users of your charging stations. It is an essential component of a successful and sustainable EV charging business.

User-Centric Messaging in EV Charging Business:

Crafting Messages for User-Centric Approach:

1. Convenience:

- Highlight the convenience your charging stations offer. Emphasize features like easy accessibility, user-friendly interfaces, and strategically located stations for maximum convenience during users' journeys.

2. Affordability:

- Communicate the affordability of your charging services. Whether it's competitive pricing, membership benefits, or discounts, underscore the cost-effectiveness of choosing your stations for EV users.

3. Sustainability:

- Showcase the sustainability aspect of your charging stations. Communicate how using your services contributes to reducing carbon footprints and supporting a greener, more sustainable mode of transportation.

4. Reliability:

- Emphasize the reliability of your charging infrastructure. Assure users that they can depend on your stations for consistent and efficient charging, reducing concerns about unexpected issues.

5. User-Friendly Experience:

- Communicate the user-friendly experience your charging stations provide. Whether it's intuitive interfaces, clear instructions, or responsive customer support, highlight elements that make the user experience seamless.

6. Fast Charging Solutions:

- If your stations offer fast charging solutions, make this a focal point. Many EV users prioritize quick charging, and messaging that emphasizes fast and efficient service will resonate with this segment.

7. Membership Benefits:

- If applicable, communicate the benefits of becoming a member. This could include exclusive discounts, loyalty programs, or access to premium features, creating additional incentives for users.

8. Environmental Impact:

- Reinforce the positive environmental impact of choosing electric vehicles and utilizing your charging stations. Users who are environmentally conscious will appreciate knowing they are making a difference.

9. Accessibility and Inclusivity:

- Highlight the accessibility of your charging stations for a wide range of users. Consideration for individuals with disabilities, diverse charging connector options, and inclusive design contribute to a positive user experience.

10. Community Engagement:

- Convey a sense of community engagement. Users often appreciate businesses that actively participate in and support the EV community. This could include events, partnerships, or initiatives that involve and benefit users.

Remember to tailor your messaging across various channels, ensuring consistency in how you communicate the user-centric benefits of your EV charging stations. This approach will resonate with your target audience and enhance the overall user experience.

Seamless User Experience in EV Charging Business:

Key Aspects to Emphasize for a Seamless User Experience:

1. Easy Payment Options:

- Highlight the simplicity of your payment process. Whether it's contactless payments, mobile app transactions, or user-friendly kiosks, emphasize the ease of completing payments at your charging stations.

2. Intuitive User Interfaces:

- Communicate the intuitive design of your charging interfaces. Users should be able to easily understand and navigate the charging process, making the experience straightforward and efficient.

3. Accessibility:

- Emphasize the accessibility features of your charging stations. Consider diverse user needs, including wheelchair accessibility, clear signage, and options for users with different charging connectors.

4. Quick Start and Stop:

- Highlight the quick start and stop capabilities of your charging stations. Users appreciate systems that allow them to begin and end charging sessions swiftly, optimizing their time.

5. Real-Time Information:

- Communicate the availability of real-time information. Whether through mobile apps or on-site displays, users should have access to information about charging status, estimated charging times, and station availability.

6. Seamless Connectivity:

- Emphasize seamless connectivity for users. This includes reliable Wi-Fi or mobile network connections to support mobile app interactions, real-time updates, and communication with customer support if needed.

7. User Support:

- Highlight the availability of user support. Let users know that assistance is readily available in case they encounter any issues, creating a sense of reliability and support throughout their charging experience.

8. Clear Instructions:

- Emphasize clear and concise instructions at each charging station. Users should easily understand how to initiate charging, what to do in case of issues, and how to conclude their charging session.

9. Compatibility:

- Communicate compatibility with a variety of electric vehicle models. Users should feel confident that your charging stations are suitable for their specific vehicle, promoting inclusivity in your user base.

10. Security Measures:

- Assure users of the security measures in place. Whether it's surveillance systems, well-lit areas, or visible security features, emphasize the steps taken to ensure their safety and the safety of their vehicles.

By focusing on these aspects in your marketing messages, you convey a commitment to providing a seamless and user-friendly experience at your charging stations, fostering positive perceptions among electric vehicle users.

Collaborative Marketing with Automakers in EV Charging Business:

Strategies for Collaborative Marketing:

1. Co-Branding Initiatives:

- Explore co-branding opportunities with automakers. This can involve incorporating both your charging station brand and the automaker's brand in marketing materials, creating a mutually beneficial partnership.

2. Joint Events and Promotions:

- Organize joint events and promotions. This could include launch events for new electric vehicle models, collaborative discount programs, or special promotions that highlight the synergy between the automaker and your charging stations.

3. Exclusive Partnerships:

- Establish exclusive partnerships with specific automakers. Offering special incentives or priority access to charging stations for customers of a particular automaker can create a sense of exclusivity and strengthen ties with that brand's user base.

4. Integrated Marketing Campaigns:

- Develop integrated marketing campaigns. Coordinate marketing efforts with automakers to create cohesive campaigns that span various channels, including social media, online platforms, and traditional advertising.

5. Incorporate Automaker Endorsements:

- Seek endorsements from automakers for your charging stations. Testimonials or endorsements from reputable electric vehicle manufacturers can significantly boost the credibility of your charging infrastructure among potential users.

6. Showcase Compatibility:

- Highlight compatibility with specific electric vehicle models. Make it known that your charging stations are optimized for the charging needs of vehicles from partnered automakers, showcasing a commitment to supporting their customer base.

7. Educational Collaborations:

- Collaborate on educational initiatives. Work with automakers to create educational content, webinars, or workshops that focus on EV adoption, charging best practices, and the benefits of utilizing your charging infrastructure.

8. Cross-Promotions:

- Engage in cross-promotional activities. This could involve featuring each other's branding on promotional materials, websites, or even co-producing content that highlights the advantages of electric vehicles and accessible charging solutions.

9. Joint Sponsorships:

- Sponsor events and initiatives together. Whether it's supporting EV-related conferences, trade shows, or community events, joint sponsorships can amplify the impact of your marketing efforts.

10. Collaborative Research and Development:

- Explore joint research and development projects. Working closely with automakers on innovative projects related to charging technology or infrastructure development can position your business as a key player in the electric vehicle ecosystem.

By forging collaborative marketing relationships with automakers, you not only enhance the visibility of your charging stations but also contribute to the overall growth and adoption of electric vehicles in collaboration with leading industry players.

Partnerships and Collaborations in EV Charging Business:

Importance and Strategies:

1. Strategic Alliances with Energy Companies:

   - Form strategic alliances with energy companies. Collaborate on initiatives that promote sustainable and renewable energy use, reinforcing your commitment to environmentally friendly charging solutions.

2. Collaboration with Municipalities:

   - Partner with municipalities for infrastructure integration. Work closely with local governments to ensure seamless incorporation of charging stations into city planning and development projects, fostering community support.

3. Joint Ventures with Tech Firms:

   - Explore joint ventures with technology firms. Collaborate on the integration of advanced technologies, such as smart grid connectivity, data analytics, and artificial intelligence, to enhance the efficiency and user experience of your charging stations.

4. Partnerships with Retail Chains:

- Form partnerships with retail chains. Install charging stations in collaboration with popular retail establishments, offering added value to their customers while expanding the accessibility of your charging infrastructure.

5. Education Initiatives with Environmental Organizations:

- Collaborate on education initiatives with environmental organizations. Join forces to raise awareness about the environmental benefits of electric vehicles and the role of sustainable charging infrastructure.

6. Integration with Automakers:

- Integrate with automakers for joint marketing initiatives. Collaborate on co-branded campaigns, events, and promotions to enhance the visibility and credibility of both your charging stations and the partnered automaker's electric vehicles.

7. Alliances with Ride-Hailing Services:

- Form alliances with ride-hailing services. Partner with companies in the ride-hailing industry to provide charging infrastructure for their electric vehicle fleets, contributing to the electrification of transportation services.

8. Cooperative Research and Development:

- Engage in cooperative research and development projects. Collaborate with universities, research institutions, and industry experts to drive innovation in charging technology, infrastructure design, and sustainability practices.

9. Public-Private Partnerships:

- Foster public-private partnerships. Collaborate with government agencies and local authorities to develop charging infrastructure projects, leveraging public funds, and support for the growth of EV adoption.

10. Networking with Industry Associations:

- Network with industry associations. Join forces with organizations dedicated to advancing electric mobility, sharing knowledge, and collectively addressing challenges to propel the EV charging industry forward.

By actively seeking and nurturing partnerships and collaborations, your charging business can benefit from shared expertise, expanded reach, and a more comprehensive approach to meeting the evolving needs of electric vehicle users and the broader community.

Collaborations with Local Businesses:

Importance and Strategies:

1. Community Integration:

- Local Business Presence: Collaborate with nearby businesses to integrate charging stations into the local community. This not only enhances the visibility of your charging infrastructure but also fosters a sense of community engagement.

2. Cross-Promotions and Discounts:

- Mutual Benefits: Offer cross-promotions and discounts. Partner with local businesses to provide incentives for users who utilize your charging stations, creating a win-win scenario that boosts foot traffic for both your charging infrastructure and the partnered business.

3. Enhanced User Experience:

- Additional Amenities: Consider partnerships that enhance the overall user experience. Collaborate with local businesses to provide additional amenities, such as discounts at nearby restaurants or exclusive deals at partnering shops, creating a more appealing charging destination.

4. Targeted Marketing Initiatives:

- Targeted Marketing: Collaborate on targeted marketing initiatives. Utilize joint advertising efforts to reach a broader audience, emphasizing the convenience of charging at your stations and the added benefits provided by nearby businesses.

5. Community Events and Sponsorships:

- Participate in Local Events: Participate in or sponsor local community events. This not only strengthens your ties with the community but also presents opportunities for collaborative efforts with neighboring businesses during these events.

6. Support for Small Businesses:

- Support Local Entrepreneurship: Contribute to local entrepreneurship. Collaborate with small businesses, supporting their growth and contributing to the economic development of the community where your charging stations are located.

7. Customized Loyalty Programs:

- Tailored Loyalty Programs: Develop customized loyalty programs. Create loyalty programs that extend benefits not only at your charging stations but also at partnering local businesses, encouraging repeated patronage from users.

8. Local Sustainability Initiatives:

- Shared Sustainability Goals: Align with local sustainability initiatives. Collaborate with businesses that share a commitment to sustainability, reinforcing the eco-friendly image of your charging infrastructure and contributing to local environmental efforts.

9. Educational Workshops and Events:

- Joint Educational Initiatives: Organize joint educational workshops. Collaborate on events that educate the local community about electric vehicles, sustainable practices, and the role of charging stations, emphasizing the positive impact of supporting local businesses.

10. Incorporate Local Flavors:

- Showcase Local Products: Showcase local products and services. Integrate elements of the local culture or products into your charging station experience, creating a unique and memorable atmosphere that reflects the character of the community.

By forging collaborations with local businesses, your charging infrastructure becomes an integral part of the community, offering not just a service but a holistic experience that contributes to the vitality and prosperity of the local area.

Integration with Navigation Apps:

Importance and Strategies:

1. Enhanced Visibility:

- Seamless Integration: Ensure seamless integration with popular navigation apps. Collaborate with app developers to include real-time information about your charging stations, making it easy for users to locate and navigate to your facilities.

2. User Convenience:

- Streamlined Experience: Prioritize user convenience. Integration with navigation apps streamlines the user experience, allowing EV drivers to plan their routes with charging station waypoints effortlessly, reducing range anxiety and enhancing confidence in your infrastructure.

3. Real-Time Availability Updates:

- Live Availability Information: Provide real-time availability updates. Integration should include features that allow users to check the current status of your charging stations, including availability, charging speed, and any additional amenities.

4. Compatibility with Multiple Apps:

- Diverse App Compatibility: Ensure compatibility with a variety of navigation apps. Recognize that users may have preferences for different navigation tools, so maximizing compatibility broadens the reach of your charging infrastructure.

5. Interactive Maps on Websites:

- Web-Based Interactive Maps: Extend integration to web-based maps. Incorporate interactive maps on your website that showcase the locations of your charging stations, offering users a convenient online platform for trip planning.

6. User Reviews and Ratings:

- Integrated User Feedback: Include user reviews and ratings. Integration with navigation apps allows users to provide feedback on their charging experience, helping to build trust and credibility among the EV community.

7. Promotional Features:

- Special Offers and Promotions: Leverage integration for promotional features. Consider collaborating with navigation app providers to promote special offers, discounts, or loyalty programs, attracting users to your charging stations.

8. Integration with Electric Vehicle Features:

- Link to EV-Specific Features: Integrate with electric vehicle features. Ensure compatibility with features specific to electric vehicles, such as estimating charging times, optimizing routes based on charging locations, and providing alerts for low battery levels.

9. Dynamic Routing for EV Users:

- Optimized Dynamic Routing: Collaborate on optimized routing for EV users. Work with navigation app developers to incorporate dynamic routing that considers charging station locations, helping users plan journeys with minimal disruptions.

10. Accessibility Information:

- Inclusive Accessibility Data: Include accessibility information. Integrate data on parking spaces, amenities, and accessibility features, making your charging stations attractive and accessible to a diverse range of users.

By seamlessly integrating your charging stations into popular navigation apps, you enhance visibility, accessibility, and user confidence, contributing to the overall success and widespread adoption of your charging infrastructure.

Corporate Partnerships for Workplace Charging:

Importance and Strategies:

1. Employee Satisfaction:

- Enhanced Workplace Benefits: Offer enhanced benefits to employees. Workplace charging programs contribute to employee satisfaction by providing a convenient solution for EV owners, supporting a positive workplace environment.

2. Corporate Sustainability Initiatives:

- Alignment with Sustainability Goals: Align with corporate sustainability initiatives. Position workplace charging partnerships as a tangible commitment to environmental responsibility, supporting corporations in achieving their green objectives.

3. Customized Charging Programs:

- Tailored Charging Solutions: Develop customized charging programs. Work closely with corporate partners to design workplace charging solutions that cater to the unique needs of their employees, considering factors like charging speed, accessibility, and billing options.

4. Employee Engagement and Awareness:

- Educational Initiatives: Conduct employee engagement programs. Raise awareness about the benefits of EVs and workplace charging through educational initiatives, workshops, and promotional campaigns within the corporate environment.

5. Incentive Programs for Employees:

- Employee Incentives: Introduce incentives for employees. Collaborate with corporate partners to implement incentive programs, such as discounted charging rates, exclusive access, or rewards for employees who choose electric vehicles.

6. Scalable Charging Infrastructure:

- Scalable Solutions: Provide scalable charging infrastructure. Tailor solutions that can grow with the increasing adoption of electric vehicles among employees, ensuring that the charging infrastructure remains efficient and accessible.

7. Seamless Integration with Workplace Facilities:

- Incorporate into Facility Planning: Work with corporations during facility planning. Ensure that the integration of workplace charging stations is seamless, with considerations for parking layouts, electrical capacity, and user convenience.

8. Cost-Sharing Models:

- Collaborative Cost-Sharing: Explore cost-sharing models. Collaborate on cost-sharing arrangements where the corporation and charging infrastructure provider share the financial responsibilities, making workplace charging more economically viable.

9. Employee Feedback Mechanisms:

- Continuous Improvement: Establish feedback mechanisms. Regularly collect feedback from employees to identify areas for improvement, ensuring that the workplace charging program meets the evolving needs and expectations of users.

10. Partnership Recognition:

- Recognition Initiatives: Acknowledge corporate partnerships. Implement recognition initiatives to highlight corporations that actively support sustainable transportation through workplace charging, fostering a positive public image for both parties.

By forging corporate partnerships for workplace charging, you not only contribute to the growth of electric mobility but also position your charging infrastructure as an integral part of corporate sustainability efforts, fostering a positive impact on both employees and the broader community.

Sponsorship of EV Events:

Importance and Strategies:

1. Brand Visibility:

- Showcasing Charging Stations: Leverage events for station visibility. Actively participate in EV-related events to showcase your charging stations, allowing attendees to experience the infrastructure firsthand and fostering brand recognition.

2. Networking Opportunities:

- Connect with Industry Stakeholders: Utilize events for networking. Sponsorship provides opportunities to connect with key stakeholders, including industry leaders, policymakers, and potential partners, fostering collaborations and expanding your network.

3. User Engagement:

- Engage with EV Enthusiasts: Target EV enthusiasts directly. Sponsorship allows you to engage with individuals passionate about electric vehicles, facilitating meaningful interactions and discussions about your charging solutions.

4. Knowledge Sharing:

- Stay Abreast of Industry Trends: Participate in conferences and exhibitions. Sponsorship offers a platform to stay informed about the latest industry trends, technological advancements, and regulatory developments, enhancing your business's adaptability.

5. Demonstration and Testimonials:

- Live Demonstrations and Testimonials: Conduct live demonstrations. Sponsorship enables you to set up interactive displays, allowing attendees to witness the efficiency and user-friendliness of your charging stations. Collecting user testimonials at events can further build credibility.

6. Educational Workshops and Seminars:

- Host Educational Sessions: Conduct informative sessions. As a sponsor, organize workshops or seminars to educate attendees about EV charging technology, address common misconceptions, and highlight the advantages of your charging infrastructure.

7. Branded Collateral and Merchandise:

- Distribution of Branded Material: Enhance brand recall. Use sponsorship opportunities to distribute branded collateral, merchandise, or informational material, reinforcing your brand presence among event participants.

8. Collaborations with Event Organizers:

- Strategic Partnerships: Collaborate with event organizers. Build strategic partnerships to ensure prominent placement of your charging stations at key locations within the event venue, maximizing visibility and user engagement.

9. Targeted Marketing at Events:

- Tailored Marketing Initiatives: Develop targeted marketing strategies. Sponsorship allows you to tailor marketing initiatives specific to the event's audience, ensuring that your messaging resonates with potential users and stakeholders.

10. Post-Event Follow-Up:

- Engage After the Event: Extend engagement beyond the event. Implement post-event follow-up strategies to maintain connections with individuals met during the event, fostering ongoing relationships and potential collaborations.

Sponsoring or participating in EV events positions your charging infrastructure at the forefront of industry developments, offering valuable opportunities for exposure, networking, and user engagement.

Loyalty Programs with EV Manufacturers:

Importance and Strategies:

1. Enhanced User Experience:

- Exclusive Benefits: Provide exclusive perks. Collaborate with EV manufacturers to offer unique benefits, such as discounted charging rates, priority access, or loyalty rewards, enhancing the overall experience for users of specific EV models.

2. Brand Loyalty:

- Building Brand Loyalty: Foster loyalty among EV users. By aligning loyalty programs with specific EV manufacturers, you create a sense of exclusivity and brand affinity, encouraging users to choose your charging infrastructure consistently.

3. Collaborative Marketing:

- Joint Marketing Initiatives: Coordinate marketing efforts. Collaborate with EV manufacturers on joint marketing campaigns to promote the benefits of using your charging stations in conjunction with their vehicles, reaching a broader audience of potential users.

4. Targeted Promotions:

- Model-Specific Promotions: Tailor promotions to specific EV models. Implement targeted promotions that align with the characteristics and specifications of particular EVs, attracting users of those models to your charging stations.

5. Innovative Incentives:

- Incentives for New Models: Introduce incentives for new model releases. Capitalize on the launch of new EV models by offering innovative incentives, such as free charging sessions or exclusive partnerships, creating excitement among users.

6. Seamless Integration:

- Integrated Charging Solutions: Ensure compatibility with manufacturer platforms. Collaborate closely to integrate your charging infrastructure seamlessly with EV manufacturer platforms, providing users with a unified and user-friendly charging experience.

7. User Education:

- Educational Collaborations: Collaborate on user education. Work with EV manufacturers to educate users about the benefits of your charging stations, charging protocols, and any unique features that enhance the charging experience.

8. Data Sharing for Improvement:

- User Behavior Insights: Share data for mutual improvement. Collaborate on sharing anonymized user behavior data to gain insights that can be used to enhance both the charging infrastructure and EV manufacturing processes.

9. Joint Events and Initiatives:

- Coordinated Events: Host joint events and initiatives. Organize events that celebrate the synergy between EVs and your charging stations, creating opportunities for user engagement and community building.

10. Feedback and Continuous Improvement:

- Collective Improvement Efforts: Work together for continuous enhancement. Establish mechanisms for feedback exchange, ensuring that both parties can contribute to the improvement of charging infrastructure and EV technology.

Collaborating on loyalty programs with EV manufacturers not only strengthens brand loyalty but also creates a mutually beneficial ecosystem that encourages the growth of electric mobility. By providing unique benefits and incentives, you contribute to the overall appeal of electric vehicles and charging solutions in the market.

Community Engagement Programs:

Benefits:

1. Positive Brand Image:

- Community Recognition: Active participation in local events and environmental initiatives enhances your brand's image as a socially responsible and community-oriented entity.

2. User Trust and Loyalty:

- Building Trust: Community engagement fosters trust. Users are more likely to trust and be loyal to a charging provider actively involved in supporting local causes and initiatives.

3. Increased Visibility:

- Local Presence: Sponsorship of events and active participation in community activities increases your visibility locally, attracting more users to your charging stations.

4. Support for Sustainable Initiatives:

- Environmental Stewardship: Involvement in environmental initiatives aligns with the sustainability goals of the EV industry, resonating well with environmentally conscious users.

5. Word-of-Mouth Marketing:

- Positive Word of Mouth: Community engagement generates positive word of mouth. Satisfied users who appreciate your commitment to the community are likely to share their positive experiences, attracting new users.

6. Brand Differentiation:

- Stand Out in the Market: In a competitive market, community engagement helps your brand stand out. It differentiates your charging business by showcasing a commitment beyond providing charging services.

Challenges:

1. Resource Allocation:

- Time and Budget: Implementing community engagement programs requires dedicated time and budget resources, which may pose challenges for small or startup charging businesses.

2. Coordination:

- Organizing Events: Organizing or sponsoring events involves coordination. Challenges may arise in ensuring smooth event execution and aligning with community expectations.

3. Impact Measurement:

- Quantifying Impact: Measuring the direct impact of community engagement on user acquisition or brand perception can be challenging, making it challenging to assess the return on investment.

4. Balancing Initiatives:

- Aligning with Values: Choosing the right causes or events that align with both your business values and community interests requires careful consideration.

5. Public Relations Risks:

- Mitigating Risks: While community engagement is generally positive, there is a risk of negative publicity if events or initiatives are not well-planned or if unexpected issues arise.

6. Sustainability of Efforts:

- Consistency: Maintaining consistent community engagement efforts over the long term may be challenging, especially as the business grows and faces competing priorities.

Overall, the benefits of community engagement in building a positive brand image and connecting with local communities often outweigh the challenges. Strategic planning, clear communication, and a genuine commitment to community well-being can contribute to successful community engagement programs.

Cross-Promotions with Sustainable Brands:

Importance:

1. Amplifying Environmental Values:

- Unified Message: Partnering with sustainable brands reinforces the commitment to environmental values. Cross-promotions amplify the message of sustainability, resonating with consumers who prioritize eco-friendly choices.

2. Expanding Reach:

- Shared Audiences: Collaborating with sustainable brands allows for exposure to each other's audiences. This shared reach can lead to increased visibility and engagement, attracting new users to your charging stations.

3. Positive Brand Association:

- Credibility Boost: Associating with other reputable sustainable brands enhances your charging business's credibility. Consumers are more likely to trust and choose services from brands aligned with shared sustainability goals.

4. Diverse Marketing Channels:

- Multi-Channel Exposure: Cross-promotions provide opportunities to leverage different marketing channels. Shared campaigns can include social media, email newsletters, and co-branded materials, reaching consumers through various touchpoints.

5. Encouraging Sustainable Practices:

- Behavioral Influence: Collaborating with sustainable brands contributes to a broader movement toward eco-friendly practices. Users may be inspired to adopt more sustainable behaviors, including choosing electric vehicles and utilizing green charging options.

6. Mutual Support:

- Strength in Numbers: Sustainable brands working together create a network of mutual support. This collaborative approach fosters a sense of unity in promoting sustainability within the business ecosystem.

7. Innovative Initiatives:

- Creative Campaigns: Joint marketing efforts with sustainable brands allow for innovative and creative campaigns. This can include unique promotions, events, or product/service bundles that capture consumer attention.

8. Educational Opportunities:

- Shared Knowledge: Collaborations provide opportunities for knowledge exchange. Sustainable brands can share insights, best practices, and educational content, contributing to increased awareness about environmentally conscious choices.

9. Customer Engagement:

- Interactive Campaigns: Joint initiatives often involve interactive campaigns that engage consumers. From co-hosted events to interactive online challenges, these promotions encourage user participation and interaction.

10. Building a Sustainable Ecosystem:

- Contributing to a Movement: Cross-promotions contribute to building a sustainable business ecosystem. By actively supporting each other, sustainable brands collectively contribute to a broader movement for environmental consciousness.

Conclusion:

Cross-promotions with sustainable brands not only amplify the impact of sustainability messages but also create a collaborative ecosystem that benefits businesses, consumers, and the environment. The synergy between brands with shared values fosters a sense of collective responsibility in promoting a sustainable future.

Public Relations Efforts:

Importance:

1. Building Positive Image:

- Media Presence: Public relations efforts help build a positive image by securing media coverage. Highlighting the environmental impact and benefits of your charging stations fosters a favorable perception among the public.

2. Storytelling for Impact:

- Success Stories: Sharing success stories, particularly those related to sustainable practices and positive user experiences, creates compelling narratives. These stories resonate with audiences and contribute to a favorable public perception.

3. Community Engagement:

- Local Community: Public relations efforts can focus on community engagement, showcasing how your charging stations positively impact the local community. This involvement enhances brand reputation and fosters a sense of connection.

4. Crisis Management:

- Proactive Communication: In times of challenges or crises, effective public relations enable proactive communication. Addressing issues transparently and promptly helps maintain trust and credibility with the public.

5. Environmental Advocacy:

- Positioning as Advocates: Public relations can position your charging business as an advocate for environmental sustainability. Engaging with media outlets on eco-friendly initiatives reinforces your commitment to a greener future.

6. Educational Campaigns:

- Informing the Public: Public relations efforts can be used for educational campaigns. Raise awareness about the benefits of electric vehicles, the importance of sustainable charging practices, and the role your stations play in reducing carbon footprints.

7. Industry Thought Leadership:

- Expert Opinions: Establishing thought leadership within the industry enhances credibility. Provide expert opinions on trends, advancements, and challenges in the electric vehicle charging sector through media channels.

8. Media Relations:

- Building Relationships: Cultivating relationships with media outlets facilitates ongoing coverage. Regularly update journalists on newsworthy events, such as station expansions, technological advancements, or collaborations, to stay in the public eye.

9. Celebrating Milestones:

- Showcasing Achievements: Use public relations to celebrate milestones. Whether it's reaching a certain number of charging stations or achieving a significant environmental milestone, share these accomplishments with the public.

10. Stakeholder Communication:

- Transparent Communication: Public relations play a crucial role in maintaining transparent communication with stakeholders. This includes users, partners, investors, and regulatory authorities.

Conclusion:

Investing in public relations efforts is instrumental in shaping public perception, maintaining positive relationships with stakeholders, and contributing to the broader narrative of sustainability in the electric vehicle charging industry. Strategic communication through media channels can elevate your charging business as a responsible and impactful player in the sustainable mobility landscape.

CHAPTER 09

FUTURE TRENDS IN EV CHARGING

Section 9.1: Emerging Technologies

1. Wireless Charging Advancements:

- Explore ongoing developments in resonant inductive coupling and radio frequency technologies.

- Discuss the potential for dynamic wireless charging on roads and highways.

- Address challenges such as efficiency, standardization, and cost-effectiveness.

2. Ultra-Fast Chargers:

- Examine advancements in ultra-fast charging, including higher power outputs and cooling technologies.

- Discuss the impact on battery health and longevity.

- Explore collaborations between automakers and charging infrastructure providers to support ultra-fast charging capabilities.

3. Battery Technology Innovations:

- Investigate developments in solid-state batteries, exploring their potential for higher energy density and improved safety.

- Discuss innovations in lithium-ion technology, such as silicon anodes and cathode improvements.

- Explore the role of next-generation batteries in addressing range anxiety and enhancing overall EV performance.

4. Smart Grid Integration:

- Delve into the integration of EV charging with smart grids for dynamic load management.

- Discuss bidirectional charging capabilities and their potential for vehicle-to-grid (V2G) applications.

- Explore the role of artificial intelligence in predicting charging demand and optimizing grid interactions.

This section provides a comprehensive overview of the latest advancements in wireless charging, ultra-fast charging, battery technologies, and smart grid integration, shaping the future of electric vehicle charging.

Wireless Charging Advancements

Wireless charging is undergoing significant advancements, with a focus on improving efficiency and expanding its application. Innovations include:

1. Resonant Inductive Coupling: Ongoing research enhances resonant inductive coupling, improving the efficiency of transferring energy wirelessly.

2. Radio Frequency Technologies: Explore developments in radio frequency technologies, enabling efficient power transfer over longer distances.

3. Dynamic Wireless Charging: Discuss the potential for dynamic wireless charging, allowing electric vehicles to charge while in motion, especially on roads and highways.

These advancements aim to make wireless charging more accessible, convenient, and seamlessly integrated into various environments, contributing to the future of electric vehicle charging.

Ultra-Fast Chargers

Advancements in ultra-fast charging represent a pivotal development in the electric vehicle (EV) charging landscape. Key aspects include:

1. Reduced Charging Times: Explore innovations enabling higher power outputs, significantly reducing charging times for EVs.

2. Feasibility for Long-Distance Travel: Examine how ultra-fast chargers enhance the feasibility of long-distance electric travel, addressing concerns related to range anxiety.

3. Cooling Technologies: Discuss innovations in cooling technologies to manage the heat generated during high-speed charging, ensuring optimal battery health.

4. Collaborations with Automakers: Explore collaborations between automakers and charging infrastructure providers to support and integrate ultra-fast charging capabilities into EV models.

These advancements play a crucial role in making electric vehicles more accessible and practical for a broader range of users, fostering the growth of sustainable transportation.

Battery Technology Innovations: Importance and Impact

1. Increased Energy Density and Faster Charging:

- Explore emerging battery technologies, such as solid-state batteries and advancements in lithium-ion chemistry, promising higher energy density.

- Discuss innovations that contribute to faster charging times, addressing one of the key challenges in electric vehicle adoption.

2. Influence on Electric Vehicle Design:

- Examine how these battery innovations influence the design and architecture of electric vehicles.

- Discuss potential weight reductions, allowing for more efficient and aerodynamic vehicle designs.

3. Extended Driving Ranges:

- Consider the impact of improved energy density on driving ranges, addressing concerns related to range anxiety.

- Discuss the potential for electric vehicles to compete with traditional internal combustion engine vehicles in terms of mileage.

4. Enhanced Performance:

- Explore how advancements in battery technology contribute to enhanced overall performance, including acceleration and power delivery.

Understanding and embracing these battery technology innovations are crucial for the continuous evolution of electric vehicles, making them more appealing, efficient, and competitive in the automotive market.

Smart Grid Integration

Smart grid integration is a pivotal aspect of advancing EV charging infrastructure. Key components include:

1. Bidirectional Energy Flow:

- Explore how bidirectional energy flow allows electric vehicles not only to consume energy but also to contribute excess energy back to the grid.

- Discuss the potential for vehicles to act as distributed energy resources, enhancing grid flexibility.

2. Smart Charging Algorithms:

- Examine the role of smart charging algorithms in optimizing charging schedules based on grid demand, pricing, and renewable energy availability.

- Discuss how these algorithms contribute to efficient and sustainable energy consumption.

3. Grid Stability:

- Explore the impact of smart grid integration on overall grid stability.

- Discuss how advanced monitoring and control systems prevent disruptions and ensure a reliable power supply.

4. Optimizing Energy Distribution:

- Consider the role of smart grids in optimizing energy distribution, minimizing wastage, and promoting a more sustainable energy ecosystem.

Understanding and implementing smart grid integration are crucial steps toward creating a more resilient, sustainable, and intelligent electric vehicle charging infrastructure.

Expansion and Scalability

Expansion and scalability are pivotal considerations for the future growth of electric vehicle (EV) charging infrastructure. Key elements include:

1. Geographical Expansion:

- Explore strategies for expanding charging networks across different regions, both urban and rural, to enhance accessibility for EV users.

- Discuss the importance of strategic placement in high-traffic areas and along major transportation routes.

2. Diversification of Charging Stations:

- Examine the potential for diversifying charging station types, including Level 1, Level 2, and DC fast chargers, to cater to varying user needs.

- Discuss the importance of offering a mix of residential, workplace, and public charging solutions.

3. Interoperability and Standardization:

- Explore efforts to standardize charging connectors and communication protocols to ensure interoperability among different charging stations and EV models.

- Discuss the importance of creating a seamless and user-friendly charging experience.

4. Integration with Other Infrastructure:

- Consider the integration of EV charging infrastructure with other urban infrastructure, such as smart city initiatives, public transportation, and parking facilities.

5. Scalable Technologies:

- Discuss the importance of adopting scalable technologies that can accommodate the increasing demand for EV charging without major infrastructure overhauls.

- Explore modular approaches that allow for the addition of charging units as demand grows.

Ensuring the expansion and scalability of EV charging infrastructure is essential for accommodating the rising number of electric vehicles and fostering widespread adoption.

Global Expansion Strategies

Global expansion in the EV charging sector involves navigating diverse markets, regulations, and infrastructure landscapes. Key considerations include:

1. Regulatory Compliance:

- Analyze how charging businesses navigate varied international regulations, standards, and compliance requirements.

- Discuss the importance of understanding and adapting to local policies governing EV charging.

2. Infrastructure Development Challenges:

- Explore challenges related to building charging infrastructure in different countries with varying levels of existing infrastructure.

- Discuss strategies for overcoming obstacles such as land acquisition, permitting, and utility coordination.

3. Market Dynamics Understanding:

- Examine how businesses tailor their approaches to align with unique market dynamics, consumer behaviors, and preferences in different regions.

- Discuss the importance of market research and adapting services to local demands.

4. Collaboration with Local Partners:

- Explore the role of partnerships with local entities, including governments, utility companies, and private businesses, in facilitating global expansion.

- Discuss the benefits of leveraging local expertise and resources.

5. Success Stories and Lessons Learned:

- Highlight success stories of EV charging businesses that have successfully expanded globally.

- Discuss lessons learned, including insights into effective strategies, potential pitfalls, and the importance of cultural understanding.

Navigating global expansion requires a nuanced approach that considers the intricacies of each market. Learning from both successes and challenges can inform future strategies for businesses aiming to establish a global presence in the EV charging industry.

Urban and Rural Scalability

Scaling EV charging infrastructure involves adapting to the unique characteristics of both urban and rural environments. Considerations include:

1. Urban Scalability:

    - Discuss the challenges and solutions for scaling charging infrastructure in densely populated urban areas.

    - Explore strategies for increasing charging station density, optimizing placement in city centers, and addressing the growing demand in urban hubs.

2. Rural Accessibility:

    - Examine the challenges of providing accessible charging solutions in less densely populated rural regions.

    - Discuss innovative approaches such as strategic placement along highways, partnerships with local businesses, and the use of renewable energy sources.

3. Balancing Demand in Urban and Rural Areas:

- Explore how businesses balance the demand for charging services in urban environments with the need for accessibility in rural areas.

- Discuss the role of data analytics and user behavior insights in optimizing charging station distribution.

4. Flexibility and Adaptability:

- Highlight the importance of flexible and adaptable infrastructure that can cater to the diverse needs of both urban and rural users.

- Discuss the role of modular designs and scalable technologies in meeting the evolving demands of different settings.

5. Community Engagement:

- Explore strategies for engaging local communities in both urban and rural areas to promote awareness and acceptance of EV charging infrastructure.

- Discuss the potential benefits of community-driven initiatives and partnerships.

Scalability in diverse environments requires a nuanced approach that addresses the specific challenges and opportunities presented by urban and rural landscapes. Businesses must adapt their strategies to ensure accessible and convenient charging options for users across varying geographic settings.

Fleet Charging Solutions

As the landscape of transportation undergoes electrification, addressing the unique needs of electric fleets becomes crucial. Explore fleet charging solutions with these considerations:

1. Evolving Fleet Electrification:

   - Discuss the growing trend of businesses transitioning their fleets to electric vehicles (EVs) for environmental and economic reasons.

   - Explore how this shift is influencing industries such as logistics, delivery services, and public transportation.

2. Tailored Charging Infrastructure:

   - Examine the specific requirements of fleet charging, including the need for high-capacity charging stations and fleet management software.

   - Discuss the challenges and solutions in deploying dedicated charging infrastructure for businesses with sizable electric fleets.

3. Operational Efficiency and Sustainability:

   - Explore the impact of fleet electrification on operational efficiency, including reduced maintenance costs and improved reliability.

   - Discuss the environmental benefits and sustainability goals achieved through the adoption of electric fleets.

4. Integration with Fleet Management Systems:

- Discuss the integration of charging infrastructure with fleet management systems to optimize charging schedules, monitor energy consumption, and enhance overall fleet efficiency.

- Explore the role of smart technologies in providing real-time data for effective fleet management.

5. Collaboration with Fleet Operators:

- Highlight the importance of collaboration between charging infrastructure providers and fleet operators.

- Discuss potential partnerships, incentives, and support mechanisms to encourage businesses to electrify their fleets.

Fleet charging solutions play a pivotal role in advancing the electrification of transportation on a larger scale. Businesses with substantial fleets can benefit from tailored charging infrastructure, contributing to both operational efficiency and environmental sustainability.

Integration with Public Transport

The integration of charging infrastructure with public transportation networks is a critical aspect of advancing the adoption of electric mobility. Explore the importance of this integration:

1. Enhanced Accessibility:

- Discuss how strategically placed charging stations at transit hubs improve the accessibility of electric public transport for commuters.

- Explore the concept of last-mile connectivity, where charging stations facilitate seamless transitions between different modes of transportation.

2. Attractiveness of Electric Public Transport:

- Highlight the role of charging infrastructure in making electric public transport more appealing to passengers.

- Discuss the potential increase in ridership when charging stations are conveniently located along major routes and at key transit points.

3. Reducing Range Anxiety:

- Address the concern of range anxiety in public transport by ensuring charging infrastructure is available at critical points in the transit network.

- Explore how the presence of charging stations can alleviate concerns about the limited range of electric public transport vehicles.

4. Operational Efficiency:

- Discuss the impact of charging infrastructure on the operational efficiency of electric public transport fleets.

- Explore how strategic charging locations can contribute to better scheduling, reduced downtime, and improved overall fleet management.

5. Integration Challenges and Solutions:

- Examine potential challenges in integrating charging infrastructure with public transport, such as space constraints and grid capacity.

- Discuss innovative solutions and technologies to overcome these challenges, including smart charging systems and grid optimization.

6. Collaboration Between Stakeholders:

- Emphasize the importance of collaboration between public transportation authorities, charging infrastructure providers, and other stakeholders.

- Discuss how collaborative efforts can lead to the successful integration of charging infrastructure into existing public transport systems.

The integration of charging infrastructure with public transport networks is a strategic move to promote sustainable and accessible transportation options. By addressing the unique needs of public transport, this integration contributes to the overall growth and acceptance of electric mobility within urban and suburban settings.

Sustainable Practices in EV Charging

Explore the key sustainable practices in the electric vehicle (EV) charging industry, emphasizing their environmental and operational significance:

1. Renewable Energy Integration:

- Discuss the growing trend of integrating renewable energy sources, such as solar and wind, into EV charging infrastructure.

- Explore the benefits of reducing carbon footprint and promoting cleaner energy consumption in the charging process.

2. Energy Storage Solutions:

- Address the role of energy storage solutions, such as advanced batteries, in optimizing the use of renewable energy for EV charging.

- Discuss how storage technologies contribute to grid stability and enable more efficient energy distribution.

3. Grid Demand Management:

- Explore strategies for demand management within the power grid to prevent overloads during peak charging times.

- Discuss the implementation of smart grid technologies and demand response systems to balance energy consumption.

4. Recycled Materials and Sustainable Design:

- Highlight the importance of using recycled materials in the construction of charging stations and associated infrastructure.

- Discuss sustainable design practices that minimize environmental impact while ensuring durability and functionality.

5. Lifecycle Assessment of Charging Equipment:

- Discuss the concept of lifecycle assessment for charging equipment, considering factors such as manufacturing, usage, and end-of-life recycling.

- Explore initiatives to design and produce charging stations with a focus on minimizing environmental impact throughout their lifecycle.

6. Community Engagement and Education:

- Emphasize the role of community engagement and education in promoting sustainable practices.

- Discuss outreach programs that inform users about the environmental benefits of EVs and sustainable charging options.

7. Government Incentives for Sustainability:

- Explore how government policies and incentives encourage the adoption of sustainable practices in the EV charging industry.

- Discuss initiatives supporting the deployment of green technologies and sustainable infrastructure.

8. Collaboration with Environmental Organizations:

- Highlight collaborations between EV charging businesses and environmental organizations to promote sustainable initiatives.

- Discuss potential partnerships that contribute to ecological conservation and climate change mitigation.

Sustainable practices in EV charging are integral to mitigating environmental impact and ensuring a responsible approach to the widespread adoption of electric vehicles. By adopting and promoting these practices, the industry can contribute significantly to a cleaner and more sustainable transportation ecosystem.

Renewable Energy Integration in EV Charging

Overview:

The integration of renewable energy sources into electric vehicle (EV) charging infrastructure marks a pivotal shift towards a more sustainable and eco-friendly transportation ecosystem. This trend involves harnessing energy from sources such as solar and wind to power charging stations, reducing reliance on conventional grid electricity. Here's a closer look:

1. Solar-Powered Charging Stations:

- Technology Implementation: Explore the installation of solar panels on or around charging stations to capture sunlight and convert it into electricity.

- Advantages: Discuss the environmental benefits of solar power, including reduced greenhouse gas emissions and decreased reliance on non-renewable energy sources.

- Case Studies: Highlight successful examples of solar-powered charging stations worldwide, showcasing their impact on local communities and the environment.

2. Wind-Powered Charging Infrastructure:

- Wind Turbines for Energy Generation: Discuss the feasibility of integrating wind turbines into charging station designs to generate clean energy.

- Advantages: Explore how wind energy contributes to sustainable charging solutions and mitigates the environmental footprint of EVs.

- Best Practices: Examine examples of wind-powered charging installations, emphasizing design considerations and efficiency.

3. Hybrid Renewable Systems:

- Combining Solar and Wind: Explore the concept of hybrid systems that combine solar and wind energy for more consistent and reliable power generation.

- Enhanced Sustainability: Discuss how hybrid systems offer a balance between energy sources, providing optimal performance in diverse environmental conditions.

- Global Applications: Highlight instances where hybrid renewable systems have been implemented successfully in various geographical locations.

4. Energy Storage Solutions:

- Integration with Batteries: Discuss the role of energy storage solutions, such as batteries, in storing excess energy generated by renewable sources.

- Grid Independence: Explore how stored energy can be utilized during periods of low renewable energy production, contributing to grid independence.

- Resilience and Reliability: Highlight the resilience and reliability benefits of incorporating energy storage into renewable-integrated charging stations.

5. Community and Environmental Impact:

- Local Benefits: Discuss the positive impact of renewable energy integration on local communities, including job creation and reduced air pollution.

- Educational Outreach: Explore initiatives aimed at educating communities about the environmental benefits of renewable energy-powered EV charging.

Renewable energy integration in EV charging not only aligns with sustainability goals but also addresses concerns related to the carbon footprint of the transportation sector. By exploring innovative technologies and sharing success stories, the industry can inspire further adoption of renewable energy solutions, contributing to a greener and more sustainable future.

Recycling and Circular Economy in EV Charging Infrastructure

Overview:

Recycling and embracing circular economy principles in the manufacturing and lifecycle management of EV charging infrastructure are integral components of sustainable practices. This approach focuses on reducing waste, reusing materials, and minimizing environmental impact throughout the entire product lifecycle. Here's a comprehensive exploration:

1. Recycling in Charging Equipment Manufacturing:

- Materials Selection: Discuss the importance of choosing recyclable and environmentally friendly materials in the manufacturing of charging stations.

- Design for Disassembly: Explore design strategies that facilitate the disassembly of charging equipment for easier recycling at the end of its lifecycle.

- Reducing Electronic Waste: Highlight initiatives aimed at minimizing electronic waste by incorporating recyclable components in charging infrastructure.

2. Circular Economy Principles:

- Product Life Extension: Discuss strategies for extending the lifespan of charging equipment, such as upgradability and modularity, to align with circular economy principles.

- Material Reuse: Explore ways in which components from decommissioned charging stations can be reused in the manufacturing of new units, reducing the demand for raw materials.

- Eco-Design Concepts: Highlight examples of eco-design principles that prioritize sustainability, energy efficiency, and recyclability in the production of charging infrastructure.

3. End-of-Life Management:

- Recycling Processes: Examine the recycling processes employed for decommissioned charging stations, including the separation and recovery of valuable materials.

- E-Waste Management: Discuss initiatives addressing the responsible disposal of electronic waste from charging infrastructure and associated electronic components.

- Certifications and Standards: Explore industry certifications and standards promoting environmentally responsible practices in the decommissioning and recycling of charging equipment.

4. Initiatives and Collaborations:

- Industry Partnerships: Highlight collaborations within the EV charging industry that prioritize recycling and circular economy practices.

- Government Regulations: Discuss the role of government regulations and policies in encouraging manufacturers to adopt sustainable practices in charging infrastructure.

5. Educational Outreach:

- Promoting Sustainability: Explore educational initiatives aimed at creating awareness about the importance of recycling and embracing circular economy principles in the EV charging industry.

- Consumer Engagement: Discuss how involving consumers in recycling programs and promoting sustainable choices can contribute to a more circular economy.

By incorporating recycling and circular economy principles, the EV charging industry can significantly reduce its environmental footprint, minimize waste, and contribute to the creation of a more sustainable and resilient charging infrastructure ecosystem.

Carbon Footprint Reduction in EV Charging Operations

Overview:

Reducing the carbon footprint in EV charging operations is crucial for promoting sustainable and environmentally friendly practices. This involves optimizing energy efficiency, minimizing emissions, and often includes offsetting initiatives to achieve carbon neutrality. Here's an in-depth exploration:

1. Optimizing Energy Efficiency:

- Advanced Charging Technologies: Explore the role of advanced charging technologies that enhance energy efficiency, such as high-efficiency power electronics and smart charging algorithms.

- Grid Integration: Discuss strategies for integrating EV charging infrastructure with smart grids to optimize energy distribution and minimize energy losses.

- Energy Storage Solutions: Highlight the use of energy storage solutions, such as batteries, to store excess energy during periods of low demand and release it during peak charging times.

2. Renewable Energy Integration:

- Solar and Wind Power: Explore the integration of renewable energy sources, particularly solar and wind power, into EV charging infrastructure.

- On-Site Renewable Installations: Discuss the implementation of on-site renewable energy installations at charging stations to generate clean energy locally.

3. Emission Reduction Strategies:

- Grid Decarbonization: Address efforts to decarbonize the electricity grid, contributing to overall emission reduction in the charging process.

- Transition to Renewable Sources: Discuss initiatives focused on transitioning charging infrastructure to rely on electricity generated from renewable sources, thus reducing reliance on fossil fuels.

4. Offsetting Initiatives:

   - Carbon Offsetting Programs: Explore the implementation of carbon offsetting programs, where emissions produced during the charging process are offset by investing in projects that reduce or capture an equivalent amount of greenhouse gases.

   - Reforestation Projects: Highlight initiatives involving reforestation projects, which absorb carbon dioxide and contribute to offsetting emissions.

5. Carbon-Neutral Practices:

   - Certifications and Standards: Discuss industry certifications and standards related to carbon-neutral practices in the EV charging sector.

   - Corporate Commitments: Explore how charging infrastructure providers and operators commit to achieving carbon-neutral operations, aligning with broader corporate sustainability goals.

6. Consumer Awareness and Education:

   - Promoting Carbon Neutrality: Discuss educational efforts aimed at informing consumers about the carbon footprint associated with different charging options and promoting carbon-neutral practices.

   - Encouraging Sustainable Choices: Explore campaigns encouraging users to choose charging stations with lower carbon footprints or those actively involved in offsetting initiatives.

Efforts to reduce the carbon footprint in EV charging operations contribute significantly to the overall sustainability of electric mobility, aligning with global initiatives to combat climate change and create a cleaner and more sustainable future.

Environmental Certifications in EV Charging Infrastructure

Introduction:

Environmental certifications play a pivotal role in ensuring that EV charging infrastructure adheres to sustainable and eco-friendly standards. These certifications contribute to transparency, accountability, and the promotion of green practices within the EV charging industry.

Importance of Environmental Certifications:

1. Transparency and Accountability:

   - Certifications provide a transparent framework that allows consumers, businesses, and stakeholders to understand the environmental impact of charging infrastructure.

   - They hold charging operators accountable for meeting specific sustainability criteria, fostering a commitment to eco-friendly practices.

2. Consumer Trust and Confidence:

- Certifications build trust among consumers by signaling that a charging station meets recognized environmental standards.

- Informed consumers, with access to certification information, are more likely to choose charging options aligned with their values, promoting sustainable choices.

3. Industry Standardization:

- Certifications contribute to the standardization of sustainable practices within the EV charging industry.

- They establish benchmarks that guide the industry toward adopting uniform environmental standards, fostering a collective commitment to reducing carbon footprints.

4. Promoting Sustainable Development:

- Certifications encourage charging infrastructure providers to adopt sustainable development practices, contributing to the long-term health of ecosystems and communities.

- They promote the integration of renewable energy sources, energy efficiency, and responsible construction practices.

5. Governmental and Regulatory Compliance:

- Certifications often align with governmental and regulatory requirements, ensuring that charging stations comply with environmental laws.

- Governments may incentivize or mandate certifications to promote sustainable practices and reduce the environmental impact of charging infrastructure.

Issuers of Environmental Certifications:

1. Green Building Councils:

- Organizations like the U.S. Green Building Council (USGBC) issue certifications like LEED (Leadership in Energy and Environmental Design) for sustainable buildings, which may include charging infrastructure.

2. Sustainable Energy Organizations:

- Entities focused on sustainable energy, such as Green-e, may issue certifications related to the use of renewable energy sources in charging operations.

3. Governmental Environmental Agencies:

- Environmental agencies at the national or regional level may issue certifications or endorse existing standards to ensure compliance with environmental regulations.

4. Independent Certification Bodies:

- Third-party certification bodies, like TÜV SÜD or Bureau Veritas, may issue certifications that verify the environmental performance of EV charging infrastructure.

Conclusion:

Environmental certifications provide a valuable framework for promoting sustainable and responsible practices in the EV charging sector. By aligning with recognized standards, charging infrastructure operators contribute to the broader goal of creating an eco-friendly and socially responsible electric mobility landscape.

CHAPTER 10

CASE STUDIES AND SUCCESS STORIES

Tesla Supercharger Network: Transforming EV Charging

Tesla's Supercharger network stands as a transformative force in the electric vehicle (EV) landscape, playing a pivotal role in accelerating the adoption of Tesla electric vehicles (EVs). Here's an exploration of its key aspects:

1. Strategic Placement:

- Tesla strategically places Supercharger stations along major highways and in urban centers, ensuring convenient access for long-distance travel and daily commuting.

- High-traffic areas and popular routes are prioritized, enhancing visibility and accessibility.

2. Scalability and Expansion:

- The Supercharger network exhibits scalability, continually expanding its coverage globally.

- Tesla's approach includes both urban and rural locations, catering to a diverse user base and facilitating long-distance travel.

3. User Experience and Efficiency:

- Tesla Superchargers are designed for speed and efficiency, offering high charging power to minimize downtime.

- The seamless user experience, facilitated by the integration of the Supercharger network with Tesla vehicles, contributes to user satisfaction.

4. Network Growth Impact:

- The extensive Supercharger network addresses range anxiety, a significant barrier to EV adoption, by providing a reliable charging infrastructure.

- It fosters user confidence, making long journeys viable and reinforcing the attractiveness of Tesla EVs.

5. Strategic Decisions and Innovation:

- Tesla's commitment to free Supercharger access for early adopters and certain models created a competitive advantage and incentivized EV purchases.

- Continuous technological innovations, such as V3 Superchargers with higher charging speeds, demonstrate a commitment to improving the charging experience.

6. Global Impact:

- The Supercharger network's global presence, spanning North America, Europe, Asia, and beyond, supports Tesla's expansion into diverse markets.

- This widespread coverage contributes to Tesla's leadership in the EV market.

Benefits:

- Overcoming Range Anxiety: The Supercharger network addresses concerns about limited EV range by providing fast and reliable charging options.

- Competitive Advantage: It contributes significantly to Tesla's competitive edge, influencing consumers to choose Tesla vehicles for their extensive charging infrastructure.

In essence, Tesla's Supercharger network stands as a driving force behind the success of Tesla EVs, showcasing the impact of a well-planned and expansive charging infrastructure on EV adoption and user satisfaction.

ChargePoint: Pioneering Charging Networks for a Sustainable Future

Evolution and Contributions:

1. Founding Principles:

- ChargePoint, founded in 2007, emerged with a vision to build the world's leading EV charging network.

- Its early focus on interoperability and open standards laid the foundation for a network that accommodates various EV makes and models.

2. Workplace Charging Prowess:

- ChargePoint's emphasis on workplace charging has been instrumental in supporting the electrification of corporate fleets.

- Workplace charging solutions foster employee EV adoption, aligning with the growing trend of companies embracing sustainability.

3. Public Charging Infrastructure:

- The expansion of ChargePoint's public charging stations addresses the needs of urban and suburban EV users.

- A user-friendly network interface and strategic placement in high-traffic areas contribute to public accessibility and user convenience.

4. Fleet Electrification Initiatives:

- ChargePoint has actively engaged in fleet electrification, catering to the needs of businesses transitioning to electric vehicles.

- Solutions for managing and optimizing fleet charging operations showcase ChargePoint's commitment to supporting sustainable transportation.

Business Model and Sustainability:

1. Open Network Model:

- ChargePoint's open network model promotes inclusivity by welcoming various EV manufacturers and fostering a collaborative approach.

- The focus on interoperability aligns with the industry's push for standardized charging solutions.

2. Aligning with Sustainability Goals:

- ChargePoint's commitment to sustainability is reflected in its efforts to facilitate the adoption of clean transportation.

- The company actively supports the transition to electric mobility as a means to reduce greenhouse gas emissions.

3. Adapting to Market Trends:

- ChargePoint's adaptability is evident in its response to market trends, including the rising popularity of electric fleets and the demand for increased charging infrastructure.

4. Smart Charging Solutions:

- ChargePoint has embraced smart charging technologies, offering features like real-time monitoring, remote management, and data analytics.

- Smart solutions contribute to efficient charging operations and enhance the overall user experience.

Impact and Future Outlook:

- Market Leadership: ChargePoint's extensive network and commitment to innovation have positioned it as a market leader in the charging infrastructure sector.

- Future Sustainability: As the EV market continues to grow, ChargePoint's role in providing sustainable charging solutions is poised to become even more significant.

ChargePoint's evolution from its founding principles to its current position as a leader in the charging infrastructure space underscores its commitment to shaping a sustainable and electric future.

IONITY: Driving High-Power Charging Across Europe

Formation and Collaborative Foundation:

1. Establishment of IONITY:

- IONITY, founded in 2017, is a joint venture between major automakers including BMW, Daimler, Ford, and the Volkswagen Group.

- The collaboration aimed to address the need for a robust high-power charging network to support long-distance EV travel across Europe.

2. Focus on High-Power Charging:

- IONITY's strategic focus on high-power charging distinguishes it as a network designed for efficient and rapid charging.

- High-power stations are capable of delivering significant charging speeds, reducing the time required for long journeys.

Network Expansion and Strategic Placement:

1. Cross-Border Expansion:

- IONITY's expansion strategy involves establishing a pan-European network, allowing seamless cross-border travel for EV users.

- The strategic placement of charging stations along major highways contributes to the accessibility and convenience of the network.

2. Key Partnerships:

- Collaboration with prominent automakers underscores IONITY's commitment to industry-wide cooperation.

- The involvement of various manufacturers ensures compatibility with a diverse range of electric vehicle models.

Challenges and Solutions:

1. Cross-Border Challenges:

   - Establishing a cross-border charging network posed challenges related to differing regulations, grid infrastructure, and local requirements.

   - IONITY navigates these challenges through strategic planning and collaboration with local stakeholders.

2. Standardization Efforts:

   - Standardizing charging infrastructure specifications facilitates interoperability and a consistent user experience.

   - IONITY's commitment to industry standards aligns with the broader goal of creating a unified and user-friendly charging network.

Impact and Future Prospects:

   - Enhancing Long-Distance Travel: IONITY's high-power charging stations contribute to making long-distance EV travel more practical and accessible.

   - Driving Industry Collaboration: The collaborative approach involving major automakers demonstrates the industry's commitment to building a comprehensive charging infrastructure.

   IONITY's success lies not only in its strategic placement and high-power charging focus but also in its ability to address cross-border challenges through collaborative efforts with key stakeholders. The venture's impact is evident in its contribution to the growth and viability of long-distance electric travel in Europe.

Strategic Site Selection: Powering EV Charging Success

Unlocking Convenience and Accessibility:

1. Traffic Patterns and High Visibility:

- Choosing locations with high traffic patterns ensures visibility and accessibility, attracting both local users and those passing through.

- Case studies reveal that charging stations strategically placed along busy routes experience higher utilization.

2. Accessibility for Urban and Suburban Users:

- A balanced approach to site selection considers both urban and suburban areas, catering to diverse user needs.

- Case studies showcase how charging networks successfully expand their reach by addressing the charging needs of users in different settings.

Case Studies in Optimization:

1. Tesla Supercharger Network:

- Tesla strategically places Superchargers along major highways and within urban centers.

- This approach maximizes convenience for long-distance travel and daily commuting, contributing to Tesla's charging network success.

2. ChargePoint's Workplace Charging Strategy:

- ChargePoint's focus on workplace charging involves collaborating with businesses to install stations where employees spend a significant portion of their day.

- Case studies demonstrate the positive impact of workplace charging in enhancing user convenience during work hours.

User Behavior Insights:

1. Understanding Charging Needs:

- Analyzing user behavior patterns helps in identifying optimal locations for charging stations.

- Case studies highlight how user-centric site selection aligns with charging needs, resulting in increased station utilization.

2. Strategic Urban Placement:

- Urban charging stations strategically located near popular destinations and shopping centers witness higher footfall.

- Successful case studies emphasize the importance of integrating charging stations into urban landscapes to encourage electric vehicle adoption.

Conclusion:

Strategic site selection forms the bedrock of a successful EV charging network. By aligning with traffic patterns, addressing urban and suburban needs, and leveraging user behavior insights, businesses can optimize site selection to enhance convenience and accessibility. Case studies underscore the real-world impact of strategic location decisions, contributing to the growth and user satisfaction within the electric vehicle charging ecosystem.

Collaborations with Local Entities: Driving EV Charging Success

Government Partnerships:

1. Collaboration with Local Governments:

- Charging businesses partnering with local governments gain support in streamlining permitting processes and adhering to regulations.

- Successful examples highlight how such collaborations contribute to the rapid expansion of charging infrastructure.

2. Incentives and Support:

- Examples showcase businesses aligning with local governments to leverage incentives and grants, fostering growth in charging infrastructure.

- Collaborations often involve shared objectives, such as promoting green initiatives, aligning business goals with public interests.

Business and Community Synergies:

1. Retail Collaborations:

- Charging stations located in collaboration with retail businesses benefit from increased foot traffic and amenities.

- Successful cases illustrate how these partnerships create a win-win scenario, enhancing the overall user experience.

2. Community Engagement Programs:

- Collaboration with local communities involves sponsoring events, supporting environmental initiatives, and integrating charging infrastructure into community spaces.

- Case studies highlight the positive impact of actively engaging with communities, fostering goodwill and building a positive brand image.

Public-Private Partnerships:

1. Public Transit Integration:

- Collaborations with public transit authorities involve placing charging stations at transit hubs, promoting accessibility.

- Examples illustrate how such partnerships contribute to the growth of electric public transportation.

2. Government-Backed Charging Networks:

- Charging businesses collaborating with government-backed initiatives witness accelerated growth and support in infrastructure development.

- Successful cases emphasize how these partnerships contribute to creating a robust and interconnected charging network.

Conclusion:

Collaborations with local entities form a cornerstone in the success of EV charging businesses. Whether through streamlined government partnerships, synergies with local businesses, or active community engagement, these collaborations contribute to enhanced visibility, operational efficiency, and sustainable growth within the dynamic landscape of electric vehicle charging. Successful examples demonstrate the potential for win-win scenarios that benefit both businesses and the communities they serve.

Innovations in User Experience: Elevating EV Charging Satisfaction

Mobile App Integration:

1. Tesla's Mobile App Ecosystem:

- Tesla's mobile app offers seamless charging experiences, enabling users to locate Superchargers, check availability, and initiate charging remotely.

- Case study analysis highlights how Tesla's user-centric app contributes to a cohesive and convenient charging journey.

2. ChargePoint's Interactive App:

- ChargePoint's app provides real-time information on charging station availability, pricing, and user reviews.

- Successful implementation showcases how user-friendly apps contribute to a positive charging experience.

Contactless Payments:

1. PlugShare's Payment Integration:

- PlugShare's platform allows users to seamlessly pay for charging sessions within the app.

- Examining this case illustrates the importance of contactless payment options in enhancing user convenience.

2. Shell Recharge's Payment Innovations:

- Shell Recharge's app facilitates easy and secure payments, eliminating the need for physical cards.

- This case study demonstrates the positive impact of streamlined payment processes on user satisfaction.

Amenities and Comfort:

1. EVgo's Charging Hubs:

- EVgo's charging hubs provide amenities like seating, Wi-Fi, and restrooms, creating a comfortable charging environment.

- Analysis showcases how amenities contribute to an enhanced user experience, making charging stations more than just a pit stop.

2. IONITY's Highway Charging Stations:

- IONITY strategically places charging stations along highways with rest areas, offering convenience and comfort during long journeys.

- This case emphasizes the importance of considering user needs for comfort and amenities in planning charging station locations.

Impact on User Satisfaction and Retention:

These case studies collectively underline the transformative impact of user-centric innovations on EV charging satisfaction and retention. Businesses that prioritize mobile app integration, contactless payments, and comfortable amenities create an environment that resonates with users, fostering loyalty and positive word-of-mouth. The success stories showcase the significance of continuous innovation in delivering exceptional user experiences within the electric vehicle charging landscape.

Charging Infrastructure Innovators: Trailblazers in the EV Revolution

1. Elon Musk - Tesla's Supercharger Network:

- Visionary Leadership: Elon Musk, CEO of Tesla, spearheaded the development of the Supercharger network, revolutionizing EV charging.

- Impact: Tesla's Supercharger network set a benchmark for fast charging, fostering EV adoption with strategic placement and high-speed capabilities.

2. Pat Romano - ChargePoint's Growth:

- Founding ChargePoint: Pat Romano, as the CEO of ChargePoint, played a crucial role in establishing one of the world's largest EV charging networks.

- Sustainability Focus: ChargePoint's commitment to sustainability aligns with Romano's vision, contributing to workplace charging and fleet electrification.

3. Michael Thwaite - Australia's EV Network:

- Founding Australia's EV Networks: Michael Thwaite is a pioneer in Australia's EV charging infrastructure, founding companies like ChargeFox.

- Expanding Reach: Thwaite's efforts focus on creating a comprehensive charging network, addressing challenges unique to Australia's vast geography.

4. Thornton Tomasetti - Wireless Charging Innovations:

- Wireless Charging Pioneer: Thornton Tomasetti, an engineering firm, explores wireless charging innovations for EVs.

- Urban Integration: Their work showcases the potential of wireless charging, especially in urban environments, promoting convenience and aesthetics.

5. Hakan Agnevall - Volvo's Charging Initiatives:

- Electrification Strategies: As President of Volvo Buses, Hakan Agnevall is driving the company's initiatives for electric buses and associated charging infrastructure.

- Sustainable Transit: Agnevall's focus on sustainable public transport showcases the importance of integrating charging infrastructure with electric fleets.

6. Erik Fairbairn - Pod Point's Residential Solutions:

- Founder of Pod Point: Erik Fairbairn played a key role in establishing Pod Point, a leading provider of residential and public EV charging solutions in the UK.

- Residential Charging Emphasis: Fairbairn's work highlights the significance of accessible and convenient residential charging solutions.

Legacy and Impact:

These innovators and companies have left an indelible mark on the EV charging infrastructure landscape. Through visionary leadership, commitment to sustainability, and overcoming challenges, they have significantly contributed to the global transition toward electric mobility. Their stories inspire the industry to continue evolving, making EV charging more accessible, efficient, and sustainable for all.

Environmental Impact Champions: Pioneering Sustainable EV Charging

1. Greenlots - Integrating Renewable Energy:

   - Leadership in Sustainability: Greenlots, a provider of charging solutions, emphasizes integrating renewable energy into its infrastructure.

   - Positive Impact: Their commitment to sustainability showcases how charging networks can contribute to a greener future.

2. Enel X - Sustainable Charging Solutions:

   - Renewable Energy Initiatives: Enel X is a global leader in sustainable energy solutions, including EV charging infrastructure.

   - Holistic Approach: Enel X's efforts demonstrate a commitment to a holistic, sustainable energy ecosystem, reducing environmental impact.

3. EVgo - Fast Charging with Clean Energy:

   - Renewable Energy Certificates: EVgo, a prominent fast-charging network, actively sources clean energy and invests in Renewable Energy Certificates (RECs).

- Clean Power Partnerships: Their dedication to clean power highlights the potential for large charging networks to be powered by renewable sources.

4. Audi - Green Charging Initiatives:

- Eco-Friendly Initiatives: Audi, as an automaker, is actively involved in promoting green charging solutions.

- E-Tron Charging Service: Audi's E-Tron Charging Service is an example of how automakers contribute to sustainable charging practices.

5. Electrify America - Sustainable Charging Network:

- Investment in Sustainability: Electrify America, with a focus on sustainable charging, has committed to investing in renewable energy projects.

- Efforts for Environmental Responsibility: Their dedication to environmental responsibility underscores the importance of sustainability in the charging industry.

6. BP Chargemaster - Carbon-Neutral Charging:

- Carbon-Neutral Operations: BP Chargemaster, a major charging network operator, has committed to making its operations carbon-neutral.

- Eco-Friendly Charging: Their initiatives showcase how charging infrastructure can align with broader sustainability goals.

Driving Change for a Greener Tomorrow:

These environmental impact champions exemplify the transformative power of sustainable practices within the EV charging industry. By prioritizing clean energy, reducing carbon footprints, and investing in eco-friendly technologies, these leaders pave the way for a more environmentally conscious future in electric mobility.

Conclusion: Shaping the Future of EV Charging

In the journey through "The Future of EV Charging," several key takeaways illuminate the transformative landscape of electric vehicle charging. From technological innovations like wireless charging to the expansion of global networks, the evolution of EV charging is redefining the automotive industry.

Key Takeaways:

1. Technological Leap: Emerging technologies, such as ultra-fast chargers and wireless solutions, promise to redefine the speed and convenience of EV charging.

2. Global Expansion: The growth of charging infrastructure globally, both in urban and rural settings, highlights the importance of accessibility for users worldwide.

3. Sustainability at the Core: Integration of renewable energy, commitment to eco-friendly practices, and environmental certifications underscore the pivotal role of EV charging in fostering sustainable transportation.

4. User-Centric Approaches: Innovations in user experience, loyalty programs, and seamless integration with daily life enhance the appeal of electric vehicles and charging infrastructure.

EV Charging: A Pillar of Sustainability:

As the automotive industry accelerates towards sustainable practices, EV charging stands as a pivotal pillar. The transition to cleaner, greener transportation is not only inevitable but also a collective responsibility. The fusion of renewable energy, technological advancements, and user-centric design positions EV charging as a catalyst for a more sustainable and eco-friendly future.

Encouragement for Entrepreneurs and Investors:

To the entrepreneurs and investors venturing into the realm of EV charging, the future holds unprecedented opportunities. The call for sustainable mobility is resonating louder than ever, and those driving innovations in charging infrastructure are at the forefront of this revolution. With a commitment to environmental responsibility and a keen understanding of user needs, entrepreneurs and investors can play a vital role in shaping the future of transportation.

Embarking on a Green Journey:

In conclusion, as we embark on this green journey, the road ahead is paved with promise. EV charging is not merely a technological advancement; it is a commitment to a cleaner, sustainable, and brighter future. Let this be an inspiration for all involved, a call to action to drive the electric revolution forward and accelerate towards a world where sustainable transportation is not just a choice but a way of life.

APPENDIX

RESOURCES AND REFERENCES

Additional Reading:

1. U.S. Department of Energy - [EV Charging Basics](https://afdc.energy.gov/files/u/publication/ev-charging-basics.pdf)

2. International Energy Agency - [Global EV Outlook](https://www.iea.org/reports/global-ev-outlook-2021)

3. Society of Automotive Engineers (SAE) - [EV Charging

Standards](https://www.sae.org/standards/ground-vehicle-standards?productTypeId=STANDARD)

4. Edison Electric Institute - [Charging Infrastructure Key Considerations](https://www.eei.org/issuesandpolicy/electrictransportation/Documents/EVchargingKeyConsiderations.pdf)

Useful Websites:

1. [PlugShare](https://www.plugshare.com/) - A platform to find EV charging stations, plan trips, and connect with other EV enthusiasts.

2. [ChargePoint](https://www.chargepoint.com/) - A leading EV charging network operator providing solutions for public, private, and fleet charging.

3. [Electrify America](https://www.electrifyamerica.com/) - A network focusing on fast-charging infrastructure across North America.

4. [InsideEVs](https://insideevs.com/) - A comprehensive source for electric vehicle news, reviews, and insights.

Glossary of EV Charging Terms:

- EVSE: Electric Vehicle Supply Equipment, commonly known as charging stations.

- DCFC: Direct Current Fast Charging, a high-power charging method that provides a faster charging rate.

- kWh: Kilowatt-hour, a unit of energy commonly used to measure the capacity of batteries or the amount of energy consumed during charging.

- V2G: Vehicle-to-Grid, a technology allowing electric vehicles to discharge electricity back to the grid.

- PID: Plug Identification, a standard to identify connectors and charging protocols.

- OCPP: Open Charge Point Protocol, an open-source communication standard for managing charging infrastructure.

- ZEV: Zero Emission Vehicle, a vehicle producing no tailpipe emissions.

- CPO: Charge Point Operator, a company that operates and manages EV charging stations.

- PHEV: Plug-in Hybrid Electric Vehicle, a vehicle with both an internal combustion engine and a plug-in rechargeable battery.

Note: The glossary provides brief definitions. For more in-depth information, refer to the respective standards and publications.